The Great Escape Retrospective

EAGLES LAST FLIGHT

Brian J. Turner

The Great Escape Retrospective

EAGLES LAST FLIGHT

Copyright

Brian J. Turner

The right of Brian J. Turner to be identified as the Author of the Work has been asserted by him in accordance with Copyright, Designs and Patents Act 1988.

ISBN 978-8-397-13810-0

Dedication

To all those who served, especially those who suffered as prisoners of war.

Contents

Gestapo Murders Near Danzig 1

North East Germany 1940 2

Prologue 3

Introduction 5

Background to 'The Great Escape' 7

The Great Escape 17

Last-minute Preparations 29

The Forgery Department – 'Dean and Dawson' 33

A Moonless Night 37

Life Behind the Wire 42

The RAF Special Investigation Branch 45

West Prussia and Danzig 52

RAF Investigation – Early Days 53

Stalag XX B / Willenberg 63

Recaptured Near Dirschau 69

Neugarten 27, Danzig Gestapo 72

RAF Investigation Progresses 73

The London Cage 78

Curiohaus Trials in Hamburg 81

Groß Trampken 84

Günther Venediger went to ground 96

The Trials of Günther Venediger 100

Not so Exemplary Justice 107

The British Prosecution of Crimes in Hamburg 109

Summary of Key Points 111

Epilogue	112
Appendix I	i
Appendix II	iv
Suggested Reading	xi
PICTURE REFERENCES	i

Gestapo Murders Near Danzig

In a forest near the modern-day city of Gdańsk, Poland, four RAF officers were murdered in March 1944. At that time, the territory was controlled by Nazi Germany and its leader, Adolf Hitler. These and other killings were carried out by the German secret police, the *Geheime Staatspolizei* more commonly known as the 'Gestapo'.

The four men murdered were not spies or saboteurs but prisoners of war. They had escaped from a camp in the German province of Silesia but they had committed no crime, as such, they should have been protected by the rules of war. Together with other RAF officers, these four airmen—two British, one Belgian and one Lithuanian—managed to escape through a tunnel from the Luftwaffe camp in Sagan on the night of 24-25 March 1944.

This mass breakout has been immortalised in film and has come to be known simply as *'The Great Escape'*. This was a highly organised and well-thought-out plan to get as many as two hundred prisoners beyond the wire—and even though only seventy-six managed to get away, it was still more than any other preceding escape attempt. The breakout involved men from many different Allied countries, who were all determined to 'make life hell for the Hun.'

When the news reached England of the brutal murders of nearly fifty RAF officers, it shocked the British people. It was a breach of the regulations of the Geneva Convention and was perhaps the worst war crime committed against Allied airmen during the Second World War. The events of that night and what unfolded afterwards are interwoven with lies, deception, conspiracy, and false truths.

From initial interrogations of suspects, investigating officers quickly realised that the murders were committed by the Gestapo, but who was responsible for giving the orders to shoot? The details of the killings were, at the time, hidden behind a sworn pact of secrecy by the Gestapo officers involved in these cold-blooded murders. The circumstances of how these four RAF officers came to be there, how they died, and who was directly responsible for their deaths, have remained largely unknown.

Despite the promises of the British Government, this crime was never fully investigated. Post-war politics made it difficult for investigators to freely conduct their enquiries. Unravelling the circumstances of the men's deaths has required research and study of both German and British archive material.

This book aims to correct popular misconceptions about the deaths of these four RAF officers and to shed light on what occurred following the mass breakout that so enraged the Nazi führer, Adolf Hitler. It aims to tell the truth of how these brave men died in a remote area of woodland so far from their homes.

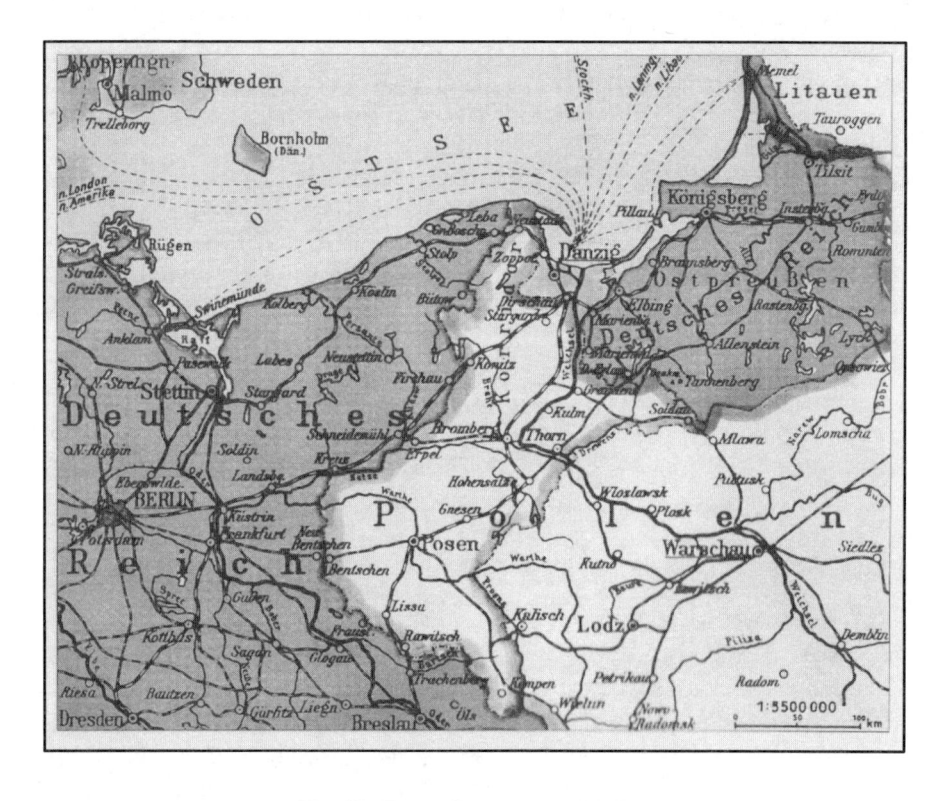

North East Germany 1940

Prologue

Near Sagan, Silesia — March 1944

The first of the young men in the tunnel hoping to escape from the prisoner of war camp climbs up the makeshift ladder to begin removing the wooden bed-boards holding up the last few inches of sandy Silesian soil. Some twenty minutes later, covered in sweat from the exertion, he is still struggling to remove the boards. This winter has been one of the coldest in Europe; the wooden boards are frozen solid in the sub-zero temperatures. A recent snowfall covered the ground above, and the damp boards are swollen by the frost making them difficult to remove. These wooden boards form the ceiling of the exit shaft, and they need to be removed urgently—some of the men have trains to catch.

Johnny Bull is finding this task far harder than he and his colleagues had anticipated; precious time is quickly slipping away, and the would-be escapers are not. All of them are packed tightly into the cramped tunnel below and they are beginning to get edgy. After half an hour, Bull comes back down the shaft, his dirt-covered face now streaked with sweat.

'Someone else will have to have a go—I'm done in,' he says with a gasp. 'Those boards have swollen up with the cold and I'm damned if I can loosen them.' He slumps exhausted against the wall of the chamber at the base of the shaft, clearly dejected.

Not wanting to waste any more time, his fellow tunneller Johnny Marshall removes his outer clothing, his escape suit tailored from his uniform, before climbing up the shaft. Working on the boards takes up more valuable time before he's able to pull one of them free. The next board comes away more easily. Once done, he makes his way back down the shaft to allow Johnny Bull back up once more to finally remove the last of the boards and break through to the surface. With renewed energy, Bull pulls down lumps of sandy soil and earth, dropping them to the floor below, where they are quickly stashed in a small dispersal chamber.

The escapers have now lost nearly two precious hours and cannot afford to lose more time. Bull works quickly removing the last of the soil and finally, the fresh cold air starts blowing down through the exit shaft and into the long length of the tunnel. This alerts the men to the progress that has been made and it eases their tension a little. Things need to move quickly now.

The plan is simple. As each man reaches the top of the ladder, Bull will put his hand on the head of the escaper, removing it only when the coast is clear. Quickly following a rope into the woods, the men will reach the marshalling point, where they will form into their escape groups.

Carrying a blanket to lie on and a coil of rope, Bull pokes his head out of the tunnel and he is shocked by what he sees.

The tunnel exit is not in the woods sheltered by trunks of pine trees but in the open ground between the wire of the camp and the woods. For some ten feet to the tree line, the men will be visible to the guards. It feels like a punch to the stomach. Instead of being hidden by the trees, there is flat snow-covered ground, which is frighteningly open. What's worse, is that there is a guard tower or 'Goon box' less than forty-five feet away. Bull can easily see the guard silhouetted against the lights of the compound; the guard's breath making clouds around his helmet in the cold night air.

Bull drops quickly back down the shaft and pushes aside the blankets leading to the exit chamber. The nervous smiles of the waiting escapers soon vanish when they see Bull's fraught expression. He whispers urgently 'We've got a problem, Roger.'

And so it begins ...

Tunnel entrance with ladder.[1]

---

[1] Muzeum Obozów Jenieckich, Żagań.

Introduction

The events of The Great Escape have been told and retold many times, originally through first-hand accounts by those who either took part or witnessed what happened during those cold winter months of 1944. With each retelling, the story changes—perhaps just a little or sometimes a great deal. With each subsequent publication, authors add their interpretations to the already existing first-hand accounts and the real story of what happened on that cold night in March 1944 gets further away from the truth.

Surely there is no intention to do this, but it is apparent that with each retelling, mistakes are made, or false information is added. Sometimes misunderstandings or misconceptions of written or oral histories serve to cloud the real history of what occurred.

Sadly, after such a long time, all of those who were involved in the escape have passed away, and it is no longer possible to clarify information or elements of the whole story directly with those who took part. With absolutely no disrespect intended, even when the 'Great Escapers' were alive, their advancing old age meant that those brave men found it increasingly difficult to recall the events of that night with clarity and accuracy. The whole experience must have been at times terrifying, men powered by adrenaline so imperfectly and indelibly created their memories. It is clear from listening to oral histories or archive recordings which were made to document their words for posterity that these were no longer young men; although engaging, from the recordings one can hear how they found it difficult to remember events with precise detail, their frail minds struggling to recall what they had said before. After the passing of so much time before the recordings were made, then this is not surprising.

Misconceptions. Were there Americans involved in the breakout? Sure, but none of them escaped on the night through the tunnel known as 'Harry'—this is an impression people have from watching the film.

Did two of those escapers carry an electric razor to keep themselves clean-shaven as they made their way on foot through Germany to occupied Poland? Obviously, this was not possible since battery-powered razors were not available until after the war. So, despite what someone may have said in an interview this could not have happened.

Did a senior British officer wear an Irish Guards uniform when he escaped? Again, this is not confirmed in that officer's account of the escape given to the investigators, nor in his post-war debriefing or any of the other contemporary accounts. Simple logic would tell us that it would have been incredibly dangerous to attract any attention when attempting to pass through an increasingly vengeful civilian German population that often vented their frustrations on downed airmen with beatings or worse.

> *'Under his heavy, belted, dyed greatcoat, Wings wore a naval officer's double-breasted jacket, the buttons covered with cloth.'* [2]

*

This book does not aim to retell the whole story, that has been done by others. However, it focuses on the last few days of four brave young men who made a bid for freedom but who were killed near Danzig. The escapers were friends, they travelled by train managing to get an impressive distance from the camp before being recaptured and handed over to the Gestapo.

This aspect of The Great Escape story is perhaps the least understood and it is possible to see mistakes being frequently repeated without any questions being asked about the logic of those supposed facts. Some of these difficulties may have arisen from the problems faced by investigators in their search for those who were responsible—but their task must have been incredibly daunting. The team encountered many difficulties in locating all of those suspected of being involved in the murders which led to problems with building a sound case against those suspects who were in custody and bringing them before the court.

Through careful analysis of archived statements, interrogations, and testimonies of the circumstances of the murders near Danzig (now Gdańsk, Poland), the author aims to honour those men—Gordon Brettell, Henri Picard, Romas Marcinkus, and Gilbert Walenn—to give them a little piece of justice by creating a more accurate account of their story.

---

[2] Sydney Smith, Wings Day (London: Collins, 1968), p153.

Background to 'The Great Escape'

As the war progressed, more and more airmen were involved in aerial combat and had the good fortune of surviving such engagements, only later to suffer the misfortune of being shot down, captured, and made prisoners of war—they were also told that for them, the war was over. Even during the early days of the war, German authorities were faced with the increasing problem of housing Allied prisoners. Initially, these were mostly Polish and many of the camps were built by their forced labour. In turn, they were joined by French and British forces following the defeat of France.

One such camp used to house prisoners of war (POWs) was Stalag Luft 3, specifically built to accommodate Allied airmen. This German prisoner-of-war camp was established in the pine forests near Sagan in Silesia, which was then part of Germany. The camp was a dismal place set in a clearing of a thick pine forest, made up of a number of barracks surrounded by high barbed wire fences.

The train station was an important transport hub, located southeast of Berlin and west of the regional capital of Breslau, and the camp was connected to both cities by the railway. At that time, Sagan station was a busy place, and noises could be easily heard from the barracks in the camp. This must have been both tempting and frustrating for the prisoners—close enough to hear the trains but separated by rows of barbed wire and armed guards that stood between them and the station, with its possibilities of freedom.

There were many such prisoner-of-war camps established in various districts of the territory controlled by the German authorities. Stalag Luft 3 was specifically built to house Allied airmen and it was controlled by the German Air Force—the *Luftwaffe*, which had airfields and training facilities nearby. Other camps for army personnel were administered by either the German army or the feared SS units. The *Schutzstaffel* was a major paramilitary organisation under Adolf Hitler and the Nazi Party in Nazi Germany, and later throughout German-occupied Europe during World War II.

Stalag Luft 3 is perhaps more famous than others. This is because of the mass breakout which took place in March 1944 and the tragic events which followed the breakout—fifty of those airmen who escaped were shot on Hitler's direct order.

The story was first documented in an account written by an Australian writer and it was published in 1950. *'The Great Escape'* by Paul Brickhill gives the reader an insider's account of the build-up to the mass breakout from the camp by British and Commonwealth airmen—however, some of the elements of the story were added or embellished perhaps for dramatic effect and included details that Brickhill may not have witnessed. However, it is still essential reading for those who want to get a first-hand eye-witness account of The Great Escape story.

Like many of his fellow airmen, Brickhill was a prisoner in the camp, he participated in the preparations for the escape but when shown the tunnel entrance he realised that due to claustrophobia, he could not jeopardise the chances of others. The tunnel was deep, very long, and with a real danger of collapsing. For many, this was just too much.

Accuracy aside, Brickhill's account of events is a valuable insight into what happened at the camp before and after the escape. The book gave the general public a better understanding of life as a prisoner of war or 'Kriegie'[3] and introduced its readers to the colourful and varied personalities involved in the escape. The book was published about the same time as the headlining court cases, during which prosecutors hoped to bring those responsible to justice, those men who were guilty of involvement in the murder conspiracy.

From the book, a dramatized version was made for the big screen with the same name. Directed by John Sturges, the film was released in 1963—on the one hand, it popularised the story of the escape but on the other, it also muddied the waters of truth by adding dramatic scenes some of which were not based on factual events. Viewers of the film will be left with the impression that American airmen escaped in German uniforms riding motorbikes, that some of them stole aeroplanes from the local airbase, and that it was an American who repeatedly escaped and spent much of his time in the camp prison referred to as the 'cooler'.

There were no Americans in the escape itself, but they had indeed played a large part in the preparations for the escape. Hence the fine character played by Steve McQueen riding a motorbike. As a tribute to those involved, some of the escapers were represented in the film using Hollywood stars which also served to guarantee the commercial success of the film. On other escape attempts it is known that escapers did steal bicycles but perhaps not motorbikes.

One fact is that a Polish airman did indeed wear a German Luftwaffe uniform as his escape disguise, which was an incredibly brave thing to do as he surely knew that discovery meant being shot as a spy. As for stealing an aeroplane, several POWs tried this on occasion, during an earlier escape from Stalag Luft 3 some of the men made

---

[3] German, Kriegsgefangener – meaning a prisoner of war.

their way to a nearby airfield but were unable to get the engine to start. As the POWs in the camp were mostly pilots it probably seemed like a good option.

Another key discrepancy between reality and fiction, one of the key dramatic scenes of the film shows recaptured officers being gunned down in a field together in a large group—this never happened. Men were murdered in pairs, small groups no larger than ten, or individually.

One can criticise the film for creating many such falsehoods about The Great Escape, but then it was never intended to be an entirely accurate historical representation of those events—in the opening frames of the film, it tells us that the characters are 'composites' and every detail is the way it happened, which isn't quite true. Many things are very accurately represented, but many details are not—such as the names of the airmen. The film has, however, kept the story of The Great Escape alive and more and more people are drawn into this amazing multi-national story of bravery, ingenuity, and ultimately its tragedy.

*

This is a true story. Although the characters are composites of real men, and time and place have been compressed, every detail of the escape is the way it really happened.

Opening titles of the Film 'The Great Escape', 1963.

Roger Bushell's Big Plan

The code name for the breakout was 'Operation Escape 200'. This bold and elaborate operation was conceived by Squadron Leader Roger Bushell, who was otherwise known as 'Big X' for his role as the leader of the Escape Committee. This code name for Bushell was very appropriate as he was big in both stature and personality in addition to being the head of the 'X' Committee. Bushell was a very driven and determined man, who was motivated by a huge desire to disrupt the German war effort in any and every way possible.

A tunnel known as 'Harry'

In the spring of 1943, Bushell masterminded the construction of three tunnels known as *Tom, Dick and Harry*; this is a phrase used commonly as 'every Tom, Dick, and Harry', meaning everyone, or 'any Tom, Dick, or Harry', meaning anyone. Again a 'codename' was used for the tunnels to prevent the guards from overhearing anything suspicious. The tunnel plan also included the production and accumulation of escape material. Other tunnelling and escape attempts were only permitted with the approval of the 'X' Committee and individual enterprises were discouraged; escape activity was 'nationalised' under one umbrella organisation.

Amongst other necessary escape items, it was necessary to produce false documents which were essential for any hope of success. Also, the introduction of layers of security and the gathering of military intelligence—some of this information was for the use of the escapers, but other useful pieces of intelligence were uncovered and sent to London in coded letters.

Essentially Roger Bushell's bold idea was to get as many as two hundred men out, if possible, through one of the three tunnels which were to be built for the scheme. The search for the escapers would tie up German forces at a time when the Allies were preparing for the invasion of Europe.

In the end, only seventy-six managed to get clear of the camp with four other less fortunate men caught either near the exit or emerging from the tunnel.

An inspiring story

Ever since the first news of the breakout and the murders which followed it reached the attention of the British public, the story gripped the public's imagination. Journalists have written many pages of news stories or magazine articles and continue to do so. The number of publications, articles, documentaries and other material produced shows that even now there is still wide public interest in the story of The Great Escape. Anniversaries may no longer host representatives from those heroes who took part or others who were held in the camp, but each anniversary is commemorated at the former location of the camp and it is also marked by articles in the popular press.

Of those seventy-six men who got away from the camp, only three managed 'home runs'; two Norwegians and one Dutchman made it back to friendly territory. Per Bergsland, a Norwegian pilot of No. 332 Squadron RAF, and Jens Müller, a Norwegian pilot of No. 331 Squadron RAF, both escaped together and made it to neutral Sweden. Jens Müller's memoir of his escape from Stalag Luft 3 was first published in Norwegian in 1946 with the title *Tre Kom Tilbake*. Müller's story was later released in English and provides a fascinating insight into the events of the escape.

Bram Vanderstok was a Dutch fighter pilot of No. 41 Squadron RAF, and he made it through Spain to Gibraltar. His memoir was first published in 1983 in his native Dutch, which was later translated and published in English in 1987.

Of those who managed to get beyond the wire, many were unable to write their memoirs as they did not survive the tragic events which followed the breakout. On the direct orders of Adolf Hitler, through Heinrich Himmler who headed the Reichs Security Office (RSHA), fifty of those recaptured were executed, in contravention of the Geneva Convention which Germany was a signatory to.

Of the remaining twenty-six, most were debriefed by British Intelligence and gave statements about their experiences. This provided essential information which was used by the RAF Special Investigation Team, and it allowed the investigators to piece together a timeline of events and thus build up a case against those involved in the murder conspiracy.

One of the senior British officers involved with the escape, Harry 'Wings' Day travelled with his Polish companion, Paweł Tobolski, and they managed to get as far as the Baltic port of Stettin before they were betrayed to the Gestapo by a French worker. His book, 'Wings Day' which was written by Sydney Smith, is an account of Day's experiences and exploits as a prisoner of war, which includes his recollections of the escape and recapture—including his later experiences of being held in Sachsenhausen.

There are many other accounts of life at the camp, there have been many books written by those who experienced captivity and other writers who have attempted to put those events into a historical context.

Moonless Night: The Second World War Escape Epic. By Bertram 'Jimmy' James. First published in Great Britain in 1983.

Lie in the Dark and Listen: The Remarkable Exploits of a WWII Bomber Pilot and Great Escaper. By Ken Rees, published in 2004.

Stalag Luft 3: The Secret Story. By Arthur A Durand First published in 1989.

These books were written to provide factual, first-hand accounts of the events. However, unfortunately, they unintentionally contain errors. Perhaps the author wrote of his experiences from memory without cross-checking certain things.

As humans, we are fallible. We don't always see things accurately and objectively. The human memory isn't exact, details fade, and memories merge. So as first-hand accounts, they are insightful, but they cannot always be relied upon for accuracy. An example of this is in Vanderstok's book he says that the tunnel known as 'Dick' was uncovered by the camp guards. Two tunnels—'Tom and Dick'—were constructed very near to each other, and as security was tight in the camp it may simply be that Vanderstok believed that it was the tunnel known as 'Dick' which was discovered by the camp guards, or 'ferrets', however, from other testimonies and the official camp history we know that this was not the case. It was the destruction of 'Tom' that so amused the Kriegies as they watched the guards use too big a charge of explosive, thereby destroying part of the barrack in the process.

Also worth considering is that it was perhaps an intensely stressful time for the airmen leading up to the escape. On the night itself, they would have been buzzing with adrenaline, weary from lack of sleep, and filled with nervous excitement at the possibility of regaining their freedom. Personal thoughts and fears would have been suppressed, so it can be no surprise that details were confused, missed or later forgotten—it would not be possible to recall everything accurately so many years later.

The Post-war Investigation into the Murders

Following the end of hostilities in Europe, a special unit was put together to investigate the circumstances of the murders with the aim track down those responsible. This investigation had also been the subject of many articles in the British and international press, together with detailed accounts in several books. Earlier works were written after interviews with some of the investigators who were directly involved or others who were witnesses to the events.

The most notable of these are the following:

Exemplary Justice. By Allen Andrews. First published in Great Britain in 1976.

A Global History of the RAF Police (The Great Escape from Stalag Luft 3) Volume 5. By Stephen R. Davies. 2012.

Human Game: The True Story of the 'Great Escape' Murders and the Hunt for the Gestapo Gunmen. By Simon Read. First published in 2013.

These accounts build on the wider story from earlier material aiming to offer new insights into the RAF investigation into the murders, detailing the reasons why some suspects were brought to justice and offering explanations as to why other high-profile perpetrators were not brought before the courts. For those interested in the details of the RAF Special Investigation they are essential reading.

Subsequent derived re-telling of the facts by established historians offer their impressions of the 'real or true story' of the escape. Maybe some of the mistakes from earlier books were corrected but equally other mistakes are repeated or indeed new ones are introduced into the mythology.

The complex story of The Great Escape and of the multi-national effort to fulfil Bushell's plan of getting as many as two hundred men beyond the wire and creating chaos in Germany is legendary—it is a story which continues to interest younger generations. Books are spawned whereby authors give their ideas of what happened and how they see things differently.

The RAF Special Investigation

After the war, a team was put together to investigate the murder of the fifty officers following the escape. The investigation was conducted under incredibly difficult circumstances, and that any of the criminals were brought to justice is a testament to the determination and dedication of the officers involved.

The chaos of war-torn Europe which had been devastated by nearly six years of conflict, together with the emerging tensions of the rapidly developing Cold War meant that it was frustratingly difficult for those involved to follow all of the leads and to conduct the investigation, particularly in the Russian-controlled areas of Germany and Poland. A supposedly allied nation was deeply suspicious of the activities of the investigators in their search for perpetrators of a crime which they considered insignificant in its scale. When the news broke of these murders it was deeply shocking for the British public and also those in POW camps at the time. However, looking at these murders in comparison with other crimes that were committed, where people were murdered in the thousands by special squads—*Einsatzgruppen*—or in the death camps intentionally built for mass murder and disposal of the victims' corpses, then it is possible to understand how the Russian authorities considered the deaths of fifty men perhaps unworthy of such a focussed investigation.

This may seem difficult to comprehend, but to illustrate this, at around the same time in occupied Poland:

- March 27 – The Germans with Ukrainian collaborators pacified the village of Smoligów in the Hrubieszów district. Estimates range from 70 to more than 200 inhabitants were murdered.
- March 29/30 – at night, a unit of the Ukrainian Insurgent Army (UPA) murdered 50 to 140 Polish inhabitants of the village of Wołczków near Stanisławów.

Pacifications of villages and mass murders were commonplace in Polish territory. When such killings took place perhaps hundreds or even thousands were murdered, and most of those crimes were never investigated.

A German Perspective on the Escape

At the time of the breakout, the camp commandant was Friedrich-Wilhelm von Lindeiner-Wildau, a German Staff Officer of the Luftwaffe. He was a Great War veteran and in his sixties when he was in command of Stalag Luft 3.

After the war, Von Lindeiner wrote his memoirs but they were not published by him at the time. This insightful account gives us a German view of what transpired, and one thing is made clear, not all Germans were National Socialists with total loyalty to the German leadership. Personal accounts written by the Kriegies themselves show that although German guards followed orders, they were not all fanatics. Indeed, as the war progressed more and more of them lost faith in the 'Final German Victory' and they became more sympathetic to the men who they were guarding.

Von Lindeiner had the rather difficult challenge of following orders but treating the prisoners well; life as a Kriegie was relatively better than that endured by other POWs, such as the concentration camps run by the SS. Von Lindeiner was aware that should any escape take place, then he and the men under his command could face court martial for their negligence of duty. Unfortunately for the commandant, the Kriegies were some of the most experienced escapers, who by this stage of their time behind the wire had amassed diverse escape experience and were now led by a very determined man who was willing to either succeed or die trying.

The camp commandant wrote his memoirs nearly fourteen years after he was dismissed from his post. They lay unread in the German Archive in Frieberg before they were discovered by Arthur Durand during research for his book. Durand went on to publish *Stalag Luft 3, the Secret Story* in 1988. One aspect of his work was the exploration of the life of Colonel Von Lindeiner, who went from camp commandant to being a post-war captive of the British.

Von Lindeiner's memoirs were eventually published in 2015; the book was authored by Marilyn Walton and Michael Eberhardt. In it, Von Lindeiner is described as a 'gentleman of the old guard, an anti-Nazi forced to please the Nazi High Command while abiding by the Geneva Convention.' He appeared to be a man struggling to adhere to his convictions and his sense of duty to the prisoners in his care. From reading the memoirs, it is clear that Von Lindeiner was both an intelligent man and also very bitter. We can read his thoughts about the escape and it gives us a valuable insight into the workings of the camp run by the Luftwaffe who were in turn forced to do the bidding of those higher up in the chain of command.

*

Other detailed information of the events can be derived from the legal cases which were prosecuted in the years just after the war.

The most famous of these cases were the Nuremberg Trials. These were held between 20 November 1945 and 1 October 1946. The International Military Tribunal (IMT) tried twenty-one of the most important surviving leaders of Nazi Germany in the political, military, and economic spheres, as well as six German organisations. The purpose of the trial was not just to convict the defendants but also to assemble irrefutable evidence of Nazi crimes. Within these trials, senior German officials were asked about their involvement in the murders of those officers who had escaped from Sagan.

Further trials were held in Hamburg which included prosecutions of some of those directly responsible for some of the killings. These are referred to as Sagan Case A and B, and the court documents are available for research in the archives. Unfortunately, from just these written accounts of events which are now so distant, it is hard to make a realistic judgement of whether someone was or was not telling the truth, or perhaps simply attempting to shift blame onto others. Many of those who were suspected of being involved with the murders were never traced, either they perished during the collapse of the Third Reich, or they managed to escape justice.

Although there were many high-profile cases and public executions of concentration camp guards, it is certainly true that many guilty persons passed into post-war society with false names and new identities. The majority of Nazis, judges, police officers, or administrative officials who had been directly involved with crimes against humanity never faced any form of justice—exemplary or otherwise.

The Great Escape

The Story of the Mass Breakout from Stalag Luft 3 – Sagan, Germany

And when I finally drew a privileged position for the actual escape, "Big X" debarred me and three or four others on grounds of claustrophobia, a correct, if infuriating, decision. A few weeks later I was deeply grateful. – The Great Escape, Paul Brickhill

The Chronicler of The Great Escape

Paul Brickhill was an Australian fighter pilot, a prisoner of war, and the author of the classic war novels *The Great Escape, The Dam Busters,* and *Reach for the Sky*. Each of these books is a story of heroism retelling real events from the war connected with the actions of members of the Royal Air Force.

Brickhill was born in Melbourne, Australia. When he was eleven years old his family moved to Sydney, where he was educated at North Sydney Boys High School. The 1930s were hard times for many, and Brickhill was forced to leave school in 1931 after his father became redundant, an effect of the Great Depression.

A school friend, Peter Finch, was working as a copyboy, and he was able to convince a news editor at The Sun to interview Brickhill in 1932. Brickhill was hired as a copyboy, and within a few years he had worked his way up to journalist, and by 1940 was a sub-editor.

World War II – The Fall of France

Brickhill was unimpressed by war fever, until the shock of France's surrender and the miracle of the British withdrawal from Dunkirk. At the same time, the young Brickhill was bored with his deskbound sub-editor job and felt a desire for adventure. He enlisted on 6 January 1941 with the Royal Australian Air Force (RAAF).

Brickhill's flight training commenced in March 1941, and then he transferred to Canada undertaking advanced training as a fighter pilot. Once completed, he was shipped to England and assigned to No. 92 Squadron RAF. The squadron was at that time equipped with Spitfires and was part of the Desert Air Force in North Africa.

On 17 March 1943, Brickhill was shot down over Tunisia but survived to become a prisoner of war. He was flown to Italy on 23 March, then sent by train to Germany. After being held at Dulag Luft, Oberursel (a town northwest of Frankfurt). At the time, this camp was a central receiving and interrogation station for captured enemy airmen, and many passed through it. The camp staff were well informed, mostly spoke English, and interrogated airmen attempting to discover any potentially useful information on military operations or new technologies being used by the RAF. Following this, Brickhill was sent to Stalag Luft 3, where he arrived in April 1943 joining his fellow airmen, some of whom were familiar to him.

By this stage of the war, escape preparations in the North Compound were well underway and Brickhill became involved with organisational duties, initially taking a role as a lookout or 'stooge', before volunteering to work as a digger on 'Tom'. During his time spent underground Brickhill developed claustrophobia, so he was unable to continue working deep underground as a digger. The committee put him in charge of security for the forgery team.

The tunnels were small, with little space to move, and tunnel collapses happened regularly. This was not a pleasant experience and it is no surprise that men like Brickhill developed claustrophobia or fear of being underground. However, these fears meant that there was a very real possibility that someone might panic during the breakout and block the escape of those behind.

Brickhill's experiences as a POW were fairly typical. Captured, taken to Dulag Luft for interrogation before being transported to a camp run by the Luftwaffe. Many of these men experienced trauma or physical injury and often had difficulties adjusting to the new reality of life within a POW camp compound. Captivity was often monotonous and a very different kind of war from what they were thus far used to—the life of a fighter pilot was filled with many emotions, fears, and physical dangers whilst life as a prisoner meant boredom, hunger, and frustration.

When it came to it, some of the men had attacks of nerves and despite the contribution they made to the preparations for the breakout, many opted to be removed from the list of escapers. Brickhill had a spot in the second hundred men and was allowed into the tunnel 'Harry' to get a feel for it. As soon as he got to the base of the entry shaft and looked along the length of the tunnel, he knew he couldn't go through with it—his claustrophobia was just too strong.

Perhaps, rather sheepishly, he went to speak with Roger Bushell and gave his reasons for asking to be removed from the list. Bushell no doubt thanked him for his honesty—if someone had panicked on the night of the breakout it would have been disastrous for those further behind them in the tunnel.

Squadron Leader Roger Bushell – 'Big X'

'Everyone here in this room is living on borrowed time. By rights, we should all be dead! The only reason that God allowed us this extra ration of life is so we can make life hell for the Hun... In North Compound we are concentrating our efforts on completing and escaping through one master tunnel. No private enterprise tunnels are allowed. Three bloody deep, bloody long tunnels will be dug – Tom, Dick, and Harry. One will succeed!' [4]

Squadron Leader Roger Bushell in his RAF uniform, before capture. [5]

---

[4] Stephen R. Davies, A Global History of the RAF Police vol 5 (Kindle: 2012), p3.

[5] Copyright: Elizabeth Carter.

Mastermind of the 'The Great Escape'

Squadron Leader Roger Joyce Bushell (30 August 1910 – 29 March 1944) was a South African-born British pilot with the RAF. Bushell was born in Springs, Transvaal, South Africa, to English parents who had emigrated there from Britain. His father was a mining engineer who used his wealth to ensure that Roger received a first-class education fairly typical of the sons of Empire men at the time. Bushell was first schooled in Johannesburg until the age of fourteen, then he went to Wellington College in Berkshire, England. In 1929, Bushell then studied Law at Pembroke College, Cambridge.

One of Bushell's primary ambitions was to fly. In 1932 he joined No. 601 Squadron Auxiliary Air Force (AAF), often referred to as 'The Millionaires' Mob' because of the number of wealthy young men who paid their way in solely to learn how to fly. Bushell was first commissioned in August 1932, before being promoted to flying officer in February 1934 and flight lieutenant in July 1936.

Although Bushell was pursuing a career with the RAF, this did not prevent him from also pursuing a legal career as a barrister-at-law. From the outset, many commented on his ability as a lawyer, particularly in criminal defence. Bushell later found himself being appointed to military cases within the RAF. Pilots were often charged with dangerous flying, and Bushell was called on to act in their defence.

During the early stage of the war, in October 1939, he successfully defended two RAF pilots, John Freeborn and Paddy Byrne, who had been charged after the friendly fire incident known as the Battle of Barking Creek. Byrne would later be held as a POW with Bushell at Stalag Luft 3.

*

Bushell was given command of No. 92 Squadron in October 1939, and promotion to squadron leader soon followed in January 1940. During the squadron's first engagement with enemy aircraft on 23 May 1940, while on a patrol near Calais, Bushell was credited with damaging two Messerschmitt Bf 110 fighter aircraft of ZG 26 before being shot down himself. He crash-landed his Spitfire, thinking it was still unoccupied France and wasn't expecting to be approached by German soldiers. It was a bitterly disappointing blow for him; however, this was the beginning of his life as a prisoner of war.

In October 1942, Roger Bushell took over control of the escape organisation at Stalag Luft 3 East Compound from Jimmy Buckley, who was at that time being transferred to another camp in Poland with many fellow officers. The camp was overcrowded, and to relieve this, men were moved to Oflag XXI B Schubin.

Bushell took over the role of 'Big X', leader of the Escape Committee, and he masterminded the scheme to construct three big tunnels known as 'Tom', 'Dick', and 'Harry'.

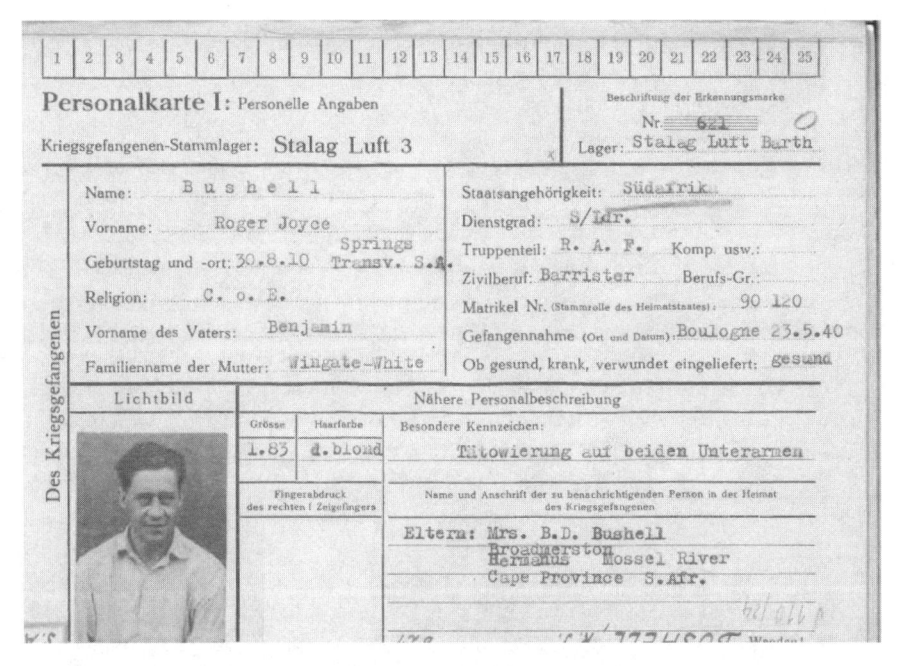

Roger Bushell's POW Card, issued by the German authorities. [6]

Early Preparations for the Escape

In the spring of 1943, prisoners were moved into the North Compound of Stalag Luft 3. It was there, that Bushell implemented plans which had already been prepared by the Escape Committee, and he became the driving force behind the scheme for a major breakout from the camp. Bushell's determination and ambition directly influenced the attitudes of others towards escaping—no private enterprise tunnels were to be allowed; all efforts were going to be focussed on 'three bloody deep, bloody long tunnels' with the conviction that one of those tunnels would succeed.

---

[6] The National Archives: WO 416/47/197

Bushell's earlier escape attempts

A fellow RAF pilot, Paddy Byrne told Bushell's parents: *'He took over the escaping organisation of Luft 3 and worked day and night to build up an organisation, the like of which had never been equalled before . . . he knew the art of being a prisoner better than most of us . . . one would think he enjoyed being a prisoner, which of course was not so, but he would not let anything get him down.'* [7]

By 1943, Bushell had spent several years in captivity and he had attempted to escape on several occasions.

In October 1941, Bushell was with other prisoners being transferred by train to Oflag VI B at Warburg, central Germany. At a brief stop in Hannover, Bushell and Czechoslovak Pilot Officer Jaroslav Zafouk jumped from the train and got away unnoticed by the guards. The pair made their way to Prague, where they made use of Zafouk's contacts, who put them in contact with the Zeithammel family—Otto Zeithammel, his son Otokar, and his daughter Blazena.

The two airmen stayed in the family apartment for nearly eight months but were betrayed by a former Czech soldier called Miroslav Kraus, who was working as a Gestapo informer. The two RAF officers were arrested and questioned at the headquarters of the secret police. Bushell was later sent to Stalag Luft 3 at Sagan, while Zafouk continued to be held in Prague. However, the Gestapo were not done with Bushell.

Reinhard Heydrich was chief of the Reich Security Main Office (RHSA—which included departments of the secret police, the criminal police, and intelligence services). Heydrich was also *Stellvertretender Reichsprotektor*—the Reich Protector of Bohemia and Moravia. Thus Heydrich was a high-ranking Nazi, a member of the SS, and a temptingly high-profile target for the Czech resistance. An attempt on his life took place in Prague on 27 May 1942, and Heydrich died a few days later on 4 June from his wounds. Bushell was taken from the camp prison at Stalag Luft 3 to Berlin for further questioning as it was suspected that he'd played a role in the organisation of the assassination attempt on Heydrich.

Bushell survived the summer of 1942, but the Nazis had plenty of reasons to shoot him—a citizen of a country at war with Germany, arrested in Prague but not in uniform, living illegally with members of the underground, and he carried Protectorate papers. The Gestapo could easily have condemned him as a spy or an agent

---

[7] Simon Pearson, The Great Escaper (London: Hodder & Stoughton, 2013), p263.

provocateur, and if he had been executed in Prague, it would have been difficult to build a prosecution case against the killers under international law.

As a senior British officer, Bushell may have been regarded as dangerous. In the Reich, there was an ever-increasing sense of paranoia that POWs could escape and join various underground organisations. These resistance movements were working against the Reich's authority. Bushell was compelled by the rules of the Geneva Convention to give nothing more than his name, rank, and number. However, under torture things may have been very different for a prisoner in such a situation.

The RSHA in Berlin released Bushell back to Stalag Luft 3 and into the camp prison known by the men as the 'cooler'. When he walked into the East Compound after his spell in solitary confinement, Bushell appeared to be a physically diminished figure. Gone was the impressive muscular definition in his chest, neck and shoulders; he looked gaunt, which can be seen in photographs from that period. None of this was surprising given that he had been interrogated by the Gestapo for three months.

Back at the camp, the case against Bushell had not been closed; it was merely on hold. Bushell had no illusions about his future—if he fell into the hands of the Gestapo again, he would be shot.

And yet, despite this Bushell's determination was not diminished. Moreover, he was now burning with an intense hatred after witnessing the terror and suffering inflicted by the Nazis in occupied Prague, and the methods used by the Gestapo first-hand. Now, he was determined to wage war from within the camp and strike back at the Germans—not a prisoner of war but a prisoner at war.

The Escape Organisation in the North Compound

As Head of the Escape Committee, Bushell's general aim was to disrupt the German war effort. He met the escape representatives of each barrack once a week and gave them an account of all escape activity. Representatives were able to discuss their ideas or the difficulties they faced. It was at these meetings that any directives about escape activity were passed to the representatives for dissemination to the personnel of their barracks.

By this stage of the war, many of the men involved with preparations for this scheme had acquired plenty of experience—whether from previous escape attempts or preparatory work for those escapes. Between them, the men had a wide and very developed range of skills. All of these would be necessary for the success of Bushell's ambitious plan.

The project management skills required were a testament to *'Bushell's power, his organisational genius and the respect with which he was held by his fellow prisoners of war.'* [8]

Many of those involved had also attempted to escape a year previously. And even though it was unsuccessful lessons had been learned.

Schubin – Oflag XXI B

This officers' camp was set up in a former school for boys near Schubin (now Szubin, Poland). In 1943, the biggest contingent was made up of British prisoners and an attempt was made to escape from the camp beneath a toilet block. All of the thirty-three officers were recaptured apart from two who sadly died at sea, it is believed that they drowned trying to cross the strait by boat between Denmark and Sweden.

One of the key learnings from this attempt was the realisation that travelling by train offered an escapee a much better chance of success. Of those men who were involved, many had travelled long distances by train whilst others who tried to get away on foot were caught soon after and often very close to the camp. Escaping by train meant a better chance of making a home run and therefore, this was repeated for the breakout from Stalag Luft 3.

It was clear to everyone that travelling by train required authentic-looking documents which the camp's forgery department would have to provide. Since it was intended for up to two hundred men to escape in one night, the camp forgers were going to be very, very busy.

---

[8] Simon Pearson, The Great Escaper (London: Hodder & Stoughton, 2013), p7.

The First Escape Committee – North Compound [9]

44879	S/Ldr. C.N.S. Campbell R.A.F., in charge of Carpentry.
42587	F/Lt. N.E. Canton R.A.F., in charge of escape food and wire-escape schemes.
	Lt. Col. Clark U.S.A.A.C., in charge of Compound Security.
90408	W/Cdr. A. Eyre R.A.F., in charge of Collation of Escape Intelligence.
J.5481	F/Lt. C.W. Floody R.C.A.F., member of Tunnel Committee.
42985	F/Lt. T.F. Guest R.A.F., in charge of Escape Clothing.
J.7755	F/Lt. G.R. Harsh R.C.A.F., in charge of Tunnel Security.
61046	F/Lt. G. Hill R.A.F., in charge of Contact Organisation.
37355	W/Cdr. G.L.B. Hull R.A.F., in charge of Labour Organisation.
	Major D. Jones U.S.A.A.C., American Escape Representative.
37321	F/Lt. R.G. Ker-Ramsay R.A.F., member of Tunnel Committee.
39103	S/Ldr. T.G. Kirby-Green R.A.F., in charge of Duty-Pilot Organisation.
89580	F/Lt. R. Marcinkus R.A.F., in charge of Escape Intelligence from Newspapers, etc.
36013	F/Lt. H.C. Marshall R.A.F., member of Tunnel Committee.
78847	F/Lt. D.L. Plunkett R.A.F., in charge of Maps.
	Lt. Cdr. N.R. Quill R.N., Advisor to Head of Committee.
37306	W/Cdr. R.R. Stanford-Tuck R.A.F., in charge of Supplies.
82532	F/Lt. E. Valenta R.A.F., in charge of 'contact' intelligence.
73023	F/Lt. G.W. Walenn R.A.F., in charge of Forgery.

*

Bushell led the organisation of all the departments which were kept very busy with the production and accumulation of escape material, the introduction of layers of security, and the gathering of military intelligence—some of which was sent to London in coded letters. The Escape Committee worked intently on their endeavours to ensure the success of the operation.

Simply, it was Bushell's charismatic leadership ability, organisational skills, and sheer determination which motivated and drove others in their efforts.

---

[9] Howard Grehan, Stalag Luft 3: An Official History of the 'Great Escape' PoW Camp (Barnsley: Frontline Books, 2016), p226.

In April 1943, Bushell called a meeting of the Escape Committee and as a former barrister, he was well aware that the opening address would be crucial to the eventual verdict, that of convincing everyone present that his plan could succeed.

'Everyone here in this room is living on borrowed time. By rights, we should all be dead! The only reason that God allowed us this extra ration of life is so we can make life hell for the Hun... In North Compound we are concentrating our efforts on completing and escaping through one master tunnel. No private enterprise tunnels are allowed. Three bloody deep, bloody long tunnels will be dug – Tom, Dick, and Harry. One will succeed!' [10]

Declaring this bold ambition to those fellow airmen in the room he not only shocked those present with its scope but injected into every man his passion and drive to put every effort into the escape plan. The simultaneous digging of three tunnels would require a huge combined effort, however, the overall plan was sound. Should one of the tunnels be discovered by the German guards then it was quite likely that they wouldn't suspect or even imagine that another two similarly elaborate and highly engineered tunnels could also be underway at the same time. This focus on three tunnels meant that no other schemes would be permitted by the Escape Committee as they might jeopardise Bushell's scheme. Anyone interested in escaping or contributing to the scheme was asked to volunteer their services.

The most radical aspect of the escape plan was not merely the scale of the construction, but also the sheer number of men that Bushell intended to pass through a tunnel on the night of the escape. Previous escape attempts had involved anything up to forty men, but Bushell proposed to get over two hundred out, the majority of whom would be wearing tailored uniforms to pass as civilian clothing and in possession of a complete range of forged papers and other escape equipment.

It was an unprecedented undertaking and required unparalleled organisation.

When hearing of the plan and the number of forged documents that would be necessary, Tim Walenn simply said 'Jesus!' To this, Bushell replied 'Maybe he'll help you.' [11]

For Walenn and the forgery team, this was a huge challenge, and he wasn't sure if it could be done; all the printing on every pass had to be hand-lettered, however, Roger was not in the mood to argue, the documents had to be ready.

---

[10] Stephen R. Davies, A Global History of the RAF Police vol 5 (Kindle: 2012), p3.

[11] Paul Brickhill, The Great Escape (New York: RosettaBooks 2000), p26.

Tom, Dick and Harry

As the men moved into the North Compound, plans which had already been made were put into place. Work began on constructing concealed entrances or 'traps' for the tunnels. In a darkened corner of a hallway in one of the barracks the entrance to 'Tom' was constructed with incredible ingenuity. The entrance to 'Harry' in hut 104 was concealed under a stove. The entrance to 'Dick' was built into a drainage sump, that was impossible to detect.

In Paul Brickhill's book, he describes the man who was given responsibility for the traps. *'Minskewitz, who was the trap expert, was a short, wiry little Polish officer in the R.A.F., with a little gray goatee beard which he was always tugging lovingly.'* [12]

This Polish officer did not act alone, he had help from his fellow Polish airmen. In the official history of the camp, written by Howard Grehan, the names of the Polish officers responsible for the traps were: F/Lt. Z. Gotowski RAF, F/Lt. L. Kozlowski RAF, and F/Lt. B. Mickiewicz RAF.

Flight Lieutenant Bronisław Mickiewicz had been a POW since August 1941. Mickiewicz led the team of ingenious Poles who constructed the traps for each of the tunnels, only one of these was ever discovered by the camp guards—otherwise known as 'ferrets'. The trap for 'Tom' was discovered by accident and it is portrayed in the film and it is one of the key dramatic scenes.

'Tom' was discovered in August 1943 when nearly complete. This forced a temporary halt in construction on 'Harry' because of security concerns but work resumed in January 1944. 'Harry' was completed in early March, and the decision was made to go on 24 March.

After many months of preparation, 'Harry' was ready, and the two hundred men selected to escape began making their final preparations.

March 1944

Last-minute preparations for the breakout were in progress but not complete. The bitterly harsh conditions of a Silesian winter posed a big danger for anyone caught outdoors for any length of time. Conditions were particularly bad, with temperatures well below freezing both day and night, it certainly wasn't a good time to escape into open country without adequate clothing. One can question whether they should have

---

[12] Paul Brickhill, The Great Escape (New York: RosettaBooks 2000), p34.

waited another month for warmer weather. However, a major consideration for the date of the escape was the very real fear of discovery. After so much preparation work, then the loss of 'Harry' would have been a devastating blow to the morale in the camp. Another concern was a possible collapse within the tunnel as the frozen ground above thawed in the warming temperatures.

With these considerations in mind, it was considered by the 'X' Committee to be too risky to delay any further. The attempt had to go ahead; no one wanted to lose the tunnel in the same way as 'Tom'.

Roger Bushell met with Len Hall the meteorological man to determine when the next moonless nights were going to be. A decision was made and the plan was finally set in motion.

Last-minute Preparations

False identity documents and travel passes

Crump turned once to see who was next and was surprised to see not a man but a suitcase. In fact, not so much a suitcase as a trunk.

Behind it grinned a strange face which he recognized after a second or two as Tim Walenn without his great mustache, which he had shaved off for the occasion.

"Where the hell d'you think you're going with this?" Crump demanded with a blend of wonder, exasperation, and amusement.

"Home, I hope," Tim said soothingly, "but I expect to the cooler, actually."

"You'll never bloody well get that thing through," Crump said.

"Don't worry. I'll cope."

"Not a hope," said Crump. "Can't be done," and they argued for a couple of minutes.

In the end Crump sent the case up on the trolley by itself, and Tim followed after. [13]

Key Figures within the 'X' Committee

The Escape Committee had been set up before the transfer from the East Compound of Stalag Luft 3. Much of the preliminary planning had already been thought through and the early stages of the project were ready to be put into action as soon as the men began to settle into the North Compound.

The first Head of the Escape Committee in the new North Compound was of course Roger Bushell or 'Big X'.

The duties of the 'X' committee were divided into various departments, such as carpentry, security, escape intelligence, etc. Of those four who escaped in the direction of Danzig, F/Lt. Romualdas Marcinkus was in charge of Military Intelligence and F/Lt. Gilbert W. Walenn was in charge of Forgery, with assistance from F/Lt. Edward G. Brettell and F/O Henri A. Picard.

Forgery was one of the key departments, with talented and resourceful artists responsible for creating the complex and wide variety of documents that were necessary for all two hundred of the escapers to carry. These documents needed to be

---

[13] Paul Brickhill, The Great Escape (New York: RosettaBooks 2000), p151.

accurate, up-to-date, and with all of the required stamps and signatures to allow each of the escapers to travel seemingly legitimately around the Reich. Without a doubt, this was one of the most crucial aspects for any hope of success in achieving a 'home run', escaping from a POW camp to friendly territory.

F/Lt. Gilbert W. Walenn

Flying Officer G W Walenn, Flight Lieutenant T L Walker (RAAF), Sergeant P A Edwards, Sergeant S C Stevens, Sergeant W A Pratt: prisoners of war; aircraft shot down and crashed off the coast of Rotterdam, Holland, Wellington N2805, 25 Operational Training Unit, 11 September 1941. [14]

Gilbert Walenn was known to the men as Tim, and he had an important role within the Escape Committee in charge of Forgery[15].

Walenn was born in Hendon, north-west London. As he grew up, Walenn inherited a love of flight from his father, who had served with the Royal Flying Corps. Before his service, Walenn worked in a London bank before enlisting in the Royal Air Force Volunteer Reserve in 1937. He was later commissioned as a pilot officer on 1 September 1939.

Serving with B Flight of No. 25 Operational Training Unit, Walenn took off in a Wellington Mark Ic bomber on the night of 10 September 1941. Early the following morning, the 'Wimpy'[16] was hit by anti-aircraft fire that crippled the aircraft and forced the five-man crew to bail out near Rotterdam. The crew of five were captured and after processing Walenn was sent to Stalag Luft 3.

A fellow Great Escaper, Flight Lieutenant Desmond Plunkett remembered it differently. In his book, he wrote that the aircraft was off course due to bad weather, and as they were running low on fuel Walenn was forced to land at an airfield in

---

[14] AIR81 Casualty File Description.

[15] Howard Grehan, Stalag Luft 3: An Official History of the 'Great Escape' PoW Camp (Barnsley: Frontline Books, 2016), p226.

[16] The Wellington bomber was known as the 'Wimpy' by airmen, after J. Wellington Wimpy from the Popeye cartoons.

occupied France. Something which he said Walenn was always rather embarrassed about.

Whichever story is true, one thing is certain, Walenn was popular amongst the other airmen and became known for his skilful drawing, as well as his enormous handlebar moustache which he grew in captivity as it was rather distinctive.

F/Lt. Romualdas Marcinkus

Pilot Officer R Marcinkus (Lithuanian): prisoner of war; Hurricane BD949, 1 Squadron; aircraft failed to return from an attack on German warships Prinz Eugen, Scharnhorst and Gneisnau (Operation Fuller) in the English Channel, 12 February 1942. [17]

Romas Marcinkus played an active role in preparations for the escape and was fluent in German. Whilst in the East Compound, he worked in the forgery department and formed a close friendship with Walenn. After the men were moved to the North compound, he was put in charge of Escape Intelligence from Newspapers.

Marcinkus was born in 1907 in the provincial Lithuanian town of Jurbarkas, which at that time was part of the Russian Empire. At age 17, Marcinkus moved from Jurbarkas to Kaunas, the temporary capital of Lithuania. There he enrolled at the Kaunas Military School, intending to enlist in the Lithuanian army. In 1932 he became a military pilot and was keen to fly in combat.

Before the outbreak of the war, Marcinkus had a very promising career as a footballer and as a playing coach for the Lithuania national football team. Sadly this passion was abandoned in favour of his hopes of playing an active role in the air.

To achieve this ambition, he travelled to France in March 1940 and requested a commission with the French Air Force. Following the German *blitzkrieg*[18] attack in May, his career in the French Air Force was cut short as France collapsed and surrendered unconditionally that same year. Rather than be captured, he first escaped to French North Africa before eventually finding passage to England. In October 1940, Marcinkus reached Liverpool, and from there travelled to London. In December

---

[17] AIR81 Casualty File Description.
[18] German, 'lightning' war.

of that year, Marcinkus became one of the many foreign pilots in the Royal Air Force, but the only Lithuanian.

*

Arriving in the port of Brest on 1 June 1940, the heavy cruiser Prinz Eugen was in urgent need of the well-equipped Brest dockyards for repairs. The cruiser had narrowly escaped a series of British naval attacks that sank her consort, the battleship Bismarck. In Brest on the French coast, her appearance alongside Scharnhorst and Gneisenau was quickly noticed by French operatives. This information was then passed on by radio to British Naval Intelligence.

Royal Air Force bombers struck eight days later, initiating a months-long air campaign against what flight crews jokingly called 'The Brest Target Flotilla.' Between August 1 and December 31, 1941, British airmen dropped 1,200 tons of bombs aimed at Scharnhorst, Gneisenau, and Prinz Eugen. This resulted in several direct hits on all three vessels and also killed or wounded over 200 seamen.

On 11 February 1942, a German operation codenamed *Cerberus* commenced, in which the squadron consisting of Scharnhorst, Gneisenau and Prinz Eugen, supported by several smaller ships, attempted to sail from Brest to their home bases by sailing through the English Channel. On 12 February, six fighters from Number 1 Squadron were tasked with intercepting these ships and the accompanying German torpedo boats. Marcinkus was one of those pilots.

Whilst attacking the Scharnhorst piloting a Hurricane IIc, Marcinkus was shot down by anti-aircraft fire and crashed into the sea. Suffering a spinal fracture during the impact, he was lucky to be rescued by the Germans, subsequently becoming a prisoner of war. After treatment, Marcinkus was sent to Stalag Luft 3, and it is believed that he was the only Lithuanian interred there.

*

The British press was scathing of its military for allowing enemy surface vessels to transit the English Channel, something that had not been accomplished for 350 years. *'Nothing more mortifying to the pride of our sea power had happened since the seventeenth century,'* scolded one editor. Some blamed Prime Minister Churchill for this, and accusations grew louder after 15 February, when news that the British bastion of Singapore had fallen to the Japanese. In perhaps the blackest week since Dunkirk, the main weight of public criticism was directed against the British Government and its leader.

During the battle, British losses were approximately forty aeroplanes. By 13 February, the ships reached their home ports, the operation had not prevented the German fleet from returning to either Kiel or Wilhelmshaven. The Times denounced the British fiasco and Prime Minister Winston Churchill ordered an inquiry.

The Forgery Department – 'Dean and Dawson'

The Forgery Department in the North Compound worked under the direction of Walenn, who had previously led the forgers' efforts in the East Compound. Many of these men had artistic backgrounds and had practised their forging skills at other camps before working on the documents required for the escape.

The Forgery Department was known as 'Dean and Dawson', named after a well-known travel agency in the UK. This practice of naming the departments after well-known British companies was a security precaution which aided in keeping their activities concealed from the guards. This practice had begun earlier in the war at Stalag Luft I where many of the POWs were previously held.

The forgery team were responsible for creating the many necessary travel documents such as identity cards and travel permits. To make things appear authentic, men were also issued with other documents like fake correspondence from girlfriends and letters from companies to show that they were travelling for work essential to the German war effort.

For the breakout, each of the escapers carried documents and passes and the creation of these was a formidable challenge for the forgery team. By the time of the escape, the forgery team created over two hundred sets of documents. Flight Lieutenant Alexander Cassie was another member of the forgery team. He was a British officer who served as a pilot on Whitley V with 77 Sqdn who had the misfortune of being shot down by a U Boat in August 1942.

Cassie decided against going out on the night of the escape and survived the war. In an interview, he revealed that it took over nine months of work to produce all of the necessary documents for each of the men. The documents were prepared and when the final decision was made by Big 'X' to go in March, all of the passes needed to be finished with signatures and dates. Once this was done, then they were committed. There was simply no possibility of delaying the escape as it would require far too long to create new sets of documents.

Tim Walenn and Romas Marcinkus knew each other and worked in the Forgery Department together. Walenn also shared a barrack room with some of the other forgers such as Desmond Plunkett (map maker), Alex Cassie, Henri Picard, and Gordon Brettell. Of those five roommates who took part in the escape—four were executed.

F/Lt. Edward G. Brettell

133 Eagle Squadron personnel; flying Spitfire aircraft detailed as bomber escort to a formation of Fortress aircraft which were to bomb Morlaix, North West France, 26 September 1942. Flight Lieutenant E G Brettell: prisoner of war, Spitfire BS313. [19]

There were many men known to have worked in the forgery department to produce the documents for the escape—amongst them was Gordon Brettell.

Brettell was born in Chertsey, Surrey. Whilst studying at university, he began a career as a motor racing driver in an Austin 7. This ambition was cut short by the outbreak of the war. Brettell enlisted in the Royal Air Force, and once his flight training was completed, he was commissioned as a pilot officer on 17 February 1941. After final training at 58 Operational Training Unit, Brettell joined No. 92 Squadron RAF flying Spitfires on 3 March 1941, which was Roger Bushell's former squadron.

Brettell was a quiet man, incredible, and likeable. '*A person as deep as the ocean itself, who I am sure I shall never quite understand. I'm very glad to have him here with me.*' [20] The words of fellow airman Neville Duke who flew with Brettell at Biggin Hill where the squadron was stationed.

In the summer of 1942, Brettell was posted to No. 133 (Eagle) Squadron RAF at Lympne as a flight commander, the only British officer within the volunteer US unit. During his service with 133 Squadron, he flew over the Dieppe beaches as top cover while the amphibious commando raid took place on 19 August. During the mission, he shot down a Focke-Wulf Fw 190 fighter.

Later that year, he led 133 Squadron on a bomber escort mission. When the flight took off, Brettell was piloting a newly built Supermarine Spitfire Mark IX fighter (serial number BS313). On 26 September 1942, the mission was to escort a group of B-17

---

[19] AIR81 Casualty File Description.

[20] Norman Franks, The War Diaries of Neville Duke (London: Grub Street 2006), p7.

bombers to Morlaix, France. Unfortunately, the entire formation was blown far off course by adverse winds. Attacks by fighters, damage from anti-aircraft fire and low fuel meant only one of the twelve aircraft of 133 Squadron made it back to England.

Brettell was captured and badly injured. After treatment, he was sent to Stalag Luft 3, where he became an enthusiastic member of the Escape Committee specialising in forged documents. He was adept at hand-producing rubber stamps from linoleum and rubber boot heels to authenticate the documents as well as fashioning embossing tools from toothbrushes.

The forgery team showed remarkable skill and ingenuity in working with limited materials. Kingsley Brown, who teamed up with the others in the forgery team, later recalled Brettell using a razor blade to carve a police department stamp from an ice hockey puck. Both Brettell and Cassie made ink from lampblack, a pigment obtained from soot mixed with oil. Cassie also had a speciality which was writing in German gothic script.

F/O Henri A. Picard

Flight Lieutenant H A Picard: prisoner of war; Spitfire BM297, 350 Squadron, aircraft failed to return from an operational flight over Abbeville, France, 27 August 1942. [21]

Also working in the forgery department, was the Belgian Spitfire pilot Henri A. Picard, who was born in Etterbeek, a suburb of Brussels, Belgium.

Picard entered the Ecole Militaire in 1936 to train as a Belgian Army officer for the Chasseurs Ardennais. During training he developed a fascination for aviation, extended his service contract in November 1937 and entered the Ecole d'Aeronautique in December 1938 to train as an air observer, graduating as a sous-lieutenant d'Aeronautique in June 1939. After the German invasion of Belgium in May 1940 the school was evacuated to France, then to Algeria and on to Morocco. On 28 June 1940, Picard and other Belgian pilots travelled to Gibraltar. From there, they sailed for England, arriving on 14 July 1940.

At RAF Gloucester Picard was commissioned pilot officer in the Royal Air Force Volunteer Reserve (RAFVR) on 8 November 1940 and completed his pilot training.

---

[21] AIR81 Casualty File Description.

Picard received his operational training in Scotland at No. 58 Operational Training Unit at RAF Grangemouth in July 1941 and in August joined No. 131 Squadron RAF in the Belgian flight.

On 14 November 1941, he was posted to No. 350 (Belgian) Squadron at RAF Valley in Wales, flying convoy escorts in Supermarine Spitfire fighters until April 1942 when they transferred to RAF Kenley for fighter sweeps over occupied France.

*

On 16 August 1942, whilst flying Supermarine Spitfire Mark Vb, Picard was on a low-level ground attack operation near Merville. During this operation, a fellow pilot crash-landed after hitting a water tower and Picard damaged his aircraft severely after striking high-tension cables. Despite the damage, he was able to pilot the aircraft home. Picard was later involved in combat supporting the amphibious landings at Dieppe on 19 August 1942 and shared in the destruction of a Luftwaffe Focke-Wulf Fw 190.

On 27 August 1942, Picard took part in a mission over Occupied France known as 'Circus 208' flying a Supermarine Spitfire Mark Vb during which he was shot down by fighters over the English Channel near Abbeville. Despite being wounded, Picard managed to bail out and parachuted into the sea. He survived adrift for almost six days before being washed up on the French coast and captured.

Following his recovery in hospital, Picard was transferred to Stalag Luft 3. During his time in captivity, he was promoted to flying officer and then acting flight lieutenant. As a meticulously skilled artist, he was a natural for the forgery department.

*

Thus, there was a group of escapers who shared the same barrack room and worked together in the Forgery Department, where they produced forged passports, movement orders, railway documentation and all manner of identity papers to allow the escapers to travel around Germany with apparent legitimacy.

These four men, Walenn, Marcinkus, Picard, and Brettell later chose to escape together. Knowing each other well they presumably felt that they could depend on each other. Either they would succeed or fail together, with the expectation of being returned to the camp should they not manage to make a 'home run', the term for a successful return to friendly territory from a POW camp.

A Moonless Night

On the night of the escape, there were many unforeseen problems. At the far end of the tunnel, the hatch took several hours to open. The boards had frozen and while Lester Bull and Johnny Marshall endeavoured to break through to the surface, many of the men were waiting behind them in the tunnel getting increasingly agitated. Once the tunnel was opened, the breakout was again hindered by an air raid which meant the electric lighting in the tunnel went out—it was connected to the camp's electricity which was turned off because of the raid. More delays resulted as men with too much clothing or large suitcases created problems. Furthermore, a tunnel collapse severely hampered their efforts to escape. As things did not proceed smoothly, only seventy-six officers managed to get away from the camp with several caught at the tunnel exit.

The mastermind of the scheme, Roger Bushell, together with his partner, the young Frenchman Bernard Scheidhauer, were among the first to leave the tunnel. They successfully boarded a train at Sagan railway station which was just twelve hundred metres from the tunnel exit. Bushell and several others were on the same train bound for Breslau, which was then the regional capital of German Silesia some two hours further east of Sagan.

Most of the escapers were in pairs, however, a few preferred to travel alone. Most of the first ten walked to Sagan station. A later group of twelve men walked to another small station nearby before boarding a train. Posing as workers on leave from a wood mill, they travelled to a small station further south where they alighted and separated mostly into pairs. After saying their goodbyes, the escapers separated and walked through the snow in different directions. All were recaptured within just a few hours.

Flight to the East

Back at the camp, when Walenn wasn't forging documents, he studied the train timetables and considered the alternative options before he put together a plan for their escape route. The plan was sound as it had worked the year before when three men had escaped from the East compound.

First, the express train to Frankfurt-an-der-Oder, then a slow train to Küstrin, followed by the express train to Dirschau, a city just south of Danzig. Then a final connection to the port of Danzig or a train further east.[22] Other escaping officers

---

[22] Oliver Philpott, Stolen Journey (London: Hodder & Stoughton 1950), p282.

would follow a similar route but crucially they chose different connections and different destinations, preferring to travel west to Stettin.

*

As more of the airmen made the short walk through the woods from the tunnel exit to the train station, they joined fellow Kriegies who were already waiting. Many felt conspicuous amongst the civilians and guards. The air raid had disrupted the schedule and what with the many delays caused in the tunnel, some of the escapers had missed their intended trains and perhaps their chance to get away quickly from the camp. If they spent too long at the station, then they were at risk of being recognised by camp personnel.

Even at that early hour, civilians were waiting either for trains or any information; there was an atmosphere of general confusion and frustration at the station. Whether they were escapers or civilians most waited anxiously, which meant that the escapers were perhaps not as conspicuous as they felt.

Two of the Norwegian contingent—Jens Müller and Per Bergsland (often referred to as Peter Rockland[23])—were bound for Frankfurt an der Oder. They had walked from the tunnel exit and were able to see the station on the other side of a fence but had difficulty locating the entrance to the subway that led to the station. When they did, there was a sign which said, 'For Wehrmacht use only', so they opted to avoid this potential problem. They followed the fence which ran alongside the tracks and found an alternative way to cross over the tracks to the station.

Müller entered the ticket office first. His efforts to buy tickets were unsuccessful as the young woman tried to explain something to him, but he couldn't comprehend what she was saying. Bergsland then entered the station, and with better luck, succeeded in buying two tickets. With these in hand, the pair made their way through the passageway to their platform. People were standing and waiting for the scheduled train which was due to leave at 2.03 a.m., and thankfully for the two airmen, it arrived just before. Müller and Bergsland got on board the train and began their journey to freedom.

Unknown to Müller and Bergsland, four other escapers also boarded the same train. Tim Walenn was paired with Romas Marcinkus; Gordon Brettell with Henri Picard. It is quite possible that with the general chaos at the station, delayed trains, nervously waiting passengers, and people emerging from the shelter, all of this

---

[23] Often European pilots who flew with the RAF changed their identities to protect family members in occupied countries, in this case Norway.

combined may have aided the escapers. All of them boarded the train and departed without incident.

Escaping in a group of four, or rather two pairs, they were travelling with documents that showed them to be foreign workers. It is believed that their cover story was that they were all Lithuanian workers returning to their place of work. Marcinkus was Lithuanian and he also spoke fluent German, so the men should have felt great confidence in their chances of success. They were heading east, perhaps intending to link up with friendly contacts known to Marcinkus.

Despite the delays and frustrations of earlier, there were now several trains carrying RAF men to Breslau, Frankfurt an der Oder, and also to Berlin.

Jens Müller described their journey in his memoir, that it wasn't an express train as it stopped at every station on the line. They had sat in the third-class carriage on the rather full train mostly surrounded by Czechs and Poles. When a German mother got on with her children, she made a fuss and insisted that other travellers made room for her to sit down in the carriage.

As the train to Frankfurt-an-der-Oder rumbled along, the four-hour journey passed without incident. At 6.00 a.m., the train duly arrived at the station, and each of the escapers stepped down onto the platform. Two of them, Müller and Bergsland, walked quickly from the train to the departures board which they studied as they considered their next move. Should they take the direct train to Stettin or an earlier train to Küstrin, where they could connect with a different train to Stettin? They agreed that rather than wait several hours at the station and risk being questioned, it would be better to keep moving.

Again, riding a slow train was a good option. They arrived in Küstrin, a large railway junction at that time, without any excitement on their journey. By now, it was the early hours of 25 March, the escapers could not have known what was happening back at Stalag Luft 3. If everything was going to plan the men were safe for about another hour. Morning roll call back at the camp was at 10.00 a.m. and their absence would be noticed by the guards if, of course, the tunnel had not already been discovered. The train bound for Stettin was due to leave at the same time, so they knew the alarm would go and things could become more difficult from that moment.

Had the tunnel already been discovered? They could expect far more intense scrutiny of their documents by railway officials or the Gestapo. Müller and Bergsland would be on the train to Stettin. The question of when the alert would be sounded must have occupied their thoughts. Could their luck hold out?

Last seen at Küstrin station

In his account of the escape, Jens Müller wrote how he sat down at a table in the waiting room with Per Bergsland. They ordered two beers and took out some sandwiches. As they were enjoying their breakfast the door opened and two familiar faces walked in. They sat down at the same table but feigned ignorance of their comrades. They also ordered two beers and when they had finished those, rose from the table and went back outside to the platforms. As they left, the pair smiled slightly and so did Müller and Bergsland, each wishing the others good luck!

The fellow escapers at the Küstrin station café were not named in the memoir, but it must have been two of the others—Walenn, Marcinkus, Picard, and Brettell. All four were travelling together and at the same station. Walenn was well known to Müller so presumably, he would have named him in his memoir. Perhaps the others were not so familiar to him and he was unable to recall the names of either Brettell or Marcinkus, therefore he decided not to name them.

*

The time passed slowly. The room was crowded with all sorts of people, soldiers and civilians. We had finished eating and sat watching the people and chatting when Pete stopped suddenly in the middle of a sentence. He looked towards the exit, turned his head calmly my way and said, 'Don't turn round. An inspector is coming towards us.'

He stubbed out his cigarette. I heard footsteps behind me, boots.

They stopped. Pete looked up, past me. I heard a commanding German voice: 'Papers, please.'

I turned round and saw a young German with a sharp face and hard eyes. Pete took out his pocket book. I did the same. I tried to keep my hand from trembling as I handed him my papers. He looked at me.

'Soldiers?' he asked.

'No,' we answered. 'Norwegian workmen.' He looked at us again and we at him. Then he read our papers. Stood without saying a word. Only read on. He looked efficient. Was the tunnel discovered? Pete and I exchanged glances.

Then again we heard the German. 'Good.' He handed us our papers, saluted and left.

We breathed more easily. But the air in the waiting room felt stifling. [24]

---

[24] Jens Müller, The Great Escape from Stalag Luft III (Barnsley: Greenhill Books, 2019), p125.

*

At ten in the morning, the train for Stettin arrived and Müller and Bergsland departed. From this moment, the stories of the two groups of escapers diverged. One pair were bound for Stettin and the other four escapers were heading east, by such choices their fates were decided.

Walenn and Marcinkus had both spent plenty of time memorising railway schedules and were aware of the trains from Küstrin station which would take them through Schneidemühl and in the direction of Danzig.

Walenn, Marcinkus, Picard, and Brettell waited a while longer and when their train arrived they boarded and began their journey towards what would be their final destination.

*

As of this point, the circumstances of the deaths of these four RAF officers became something of a mystery which the team from the RAF Special Investigation Branch had to piece together—mostly from interviews with guilty men who were concerned about their fates, those men who had been involved in the murder conspiracy.

Life Behind the Wire

It was not true for all prisoners of war, but for officers, it was considered their duty to attempt to escape. Bound by the Geneva Convention, commissioned officers could not be forced to work which left them with plenty of time on their hands. Attempting to escape and the preparations for those attempts helped to pass the time and if nothing else a way to relieve boredom. Many of these officers were young, eager and keen to cause trouble for the guards whom they viewed as the enemy. In Kriegie slang, the guards were known as 'Goons'[25] and this behaviour was referred to as 'Goon-baiting' by the men who had not long before been in public schools where such boisterous mischief would have been normal.

Some of the senior officers took a dim view of this kind of activity. The camp guards who were tasked with searching out any suspicious escape activity were known as 'ferrets', and on occasions, their well-being was endangered. The death of a guard would have resulted in serious reprisals. For some of the men, Goon-baiting was a fun way of relieving tension but often resulted in making the lives of others in the camp more difficult as guards withheld mail or Red Cross parcels as punishment. Men desperately needed these parcels to supplement the meagre rations which they received.

For those who indulged in Goon-baiting, it was for them an outlet for frustration and an antidote to despair. Any opportunity to make the guards look foolish was a great morale-builder for the prisoners.

*

When the well-known fighter ace Douglas Bader arrived at Stalag Luft 3, he held hopes of escaping. As time went on his hopes began to fade, together with his time as a fighter pilot, which also receded into the past. Even if he could have escaped, he was well aware of how conspicuous he looked. Having lost the lower parts of both legs, his false limbs gave him a distinctive way of walking which easily distinguished him from others. He felt trapped.

Inevitably his frustrations were taken out on the camp guards. He indulged in Goon-baiting and scores of admirers followed his example. On one occasion, the Germans ordered all window shutters closed at dusk. Bader then instructed the men to tear them all off and throw them into the middle of the compound. This prompted a violent argument with Harry 'Wings' Day, who was a senior British officer working

---

[25] The POWs told guards that it stood for 'German Officer Or Non-com'.

on escape activity with Bushell. Day was in an awkward position, he wanted to tear the shutters off, but he also realised the importance of keeping the Germans reasonably placated so prisoners could retain privileges. He put a firm foot down about the shutters and put an end to some of the Goon-baiting.

> *Camp opinion divided; there were the turbulent rebels devoted to Bader who believed in riling the Germans at every chance, some who wanted only peace and others, the wise cool heads, who wanted a judicious amount of Goon-baiting mixed with enough tact and co-operation to ensure peace for escape work.* [26]

*

Many of the POWs had no desire to escape, preferring to aid the efforts of others. The men had suffered traumatic experiences—being shot down, loss of friends, mistreatment by civilians, and some felt shame in being a prisoner of war.

Determined escapers were a fairly small minority of men who made great demands on the camp's resources and brought hardship to all of the POWs through the inevitable German retaliation that followed any escape attempt. Many ambivalently accepted that it was their duty to resist, and even if they were not willing to be active escapers themselves, they were willing to aid in escape activity.

Some considered the whole enterprise as a 'form of escapism' because the chances of getting back to England were so small. Perhaps they felt it was their duty to escape or to try continually to do so, and in that way to distract the enemy and tie down large numbers of men. Others felt differently, they had already taken enough risks for King and Country and that it was a miracle they had survived. There was also a feeling amongst some of the men that there were others at home, both in and out of uniform, who were doing quite nicely out of the war.

Of almost six hundred men involved with the preparations for the mass breakout in March 1944, only two hundred were either selected or picked at random by lots. Men who spoke German, who made significant contributions to the organising of the escape attempt, and who were considered to have the best chance of making a 'home run' were selected. They were given priority, the first into the tunnel, together with money and passes for travel by train. Of the others who had aided in the preparations for the escape, their names were drawn at random but most had to travel on foot—known to the Kriegies as 'hardarsing'.

---

[26] Paul Brickhill, Reach for the Sky (Ballantine Books, 1967), p247.

Of those chosen, less than half made it through the tunnel on the night of the escape, which perhaps many considered a blessing in hindsight.

*

Throughout the prison camps of Europe where Allied prisoners of war were held, escape attempts were typically doomed to failure, very few prisoners managed to make a 'home run'. Many POWs died either in escape attempts or simply disappeared somewhere within Nazi Germany. The majority were recaptured and returned to the camps, and this is what most of the men who escaped from Sagan expected to happen to them if they were caught—to be returned, followed by a few weeks in the cooler.

For some, such as Roger Bushell, anything the men could do to cause disruption or chaos in Germany allowed them to feel as if they were aiding the Allied war effort. The German authorities had to expend considerable resources to keep the men captive and recover those who were on the run. With the increasing number of prisoners and foreign workers in Germany, there was also a growing paranoia that such bright and capable officers could escape and join up with resistance groups. Although the overall numbers were small some members of the British armed forces did manage to escape and give aid to the Polish Home Army.

Of the seventy-six men who escaped from Stalag Luft 3, all but three were tracked down and recaptured, and most of them within 48 hours. When Adolf Hitler heard of yet another mass breakout, he was enraged. *Reichsführer* Heinrich Himmler, *Reichsmarschall* Herman Göring and Field Marshall Wilhelm Keitel were all present at the meeting and immediately began to argue as to who was responsible for allowing such a large number of prisoners to escape. The charge was refuted by Keitel, who declared that his command had nothing to do with the camp and that responsibility lay with Göring, as the camp was run by the Luftwaffe. According to many accounts, an infuriated Hitler stopped the bickering by issuing a very straightforward order: all those recaptured should be shot.[27]

Hitler's anger was also directed at those who had allowed it to happen. He also called for the camp commandant and all guards who were on duty at the time to be court-martialled. The order to shoot all of the escapers was moderated, perhaps by Göring or Keitel, and a decision was made by the German High Command on the highest authority to execute 'more than half' of the recaptured officers as a deterrent to further escape attempts.

---

[27] WO 235/425; GWDN 1812.

The RAF Special Investigation Branch

For a full year the British authorities did not know where to place responsibility for these acts, but seventeen months after the crimes were committed the order to seek out an unknown number of unidentified murderers was issued to the Royal Air Force. The trail was cold, the terrain vast. [28]

After the end of hostilities in Europe, a special team was set up by the RAF and tasked with investigating the events of the mass breakout and the circumstances of the deaths of the fifty RAF officers.

The Royal Air Force Police Special Investigation Branch (SIB) was formed in 1918 and has the distinction of being the only branch-specific investigative unit entrusted with a major war crime. Five officers and fourteen NCOs were given the assignment of investigating the circumstances of the breakout and tasked with bringing those responsible to the exemplary justice which Eden had promised would befall those involved in the murder conspiracy.

The Beginning of the Investigation

In December 1944, Flight Lieutenant Wilfred Bowes applied to take a new appointment at the headquarters of the Royal Air Force Special Investigation Branch in Princes Gate Court, which was a commandeered block of flats in Exhibition Road, South Kensington.

Bowes was described as a stocky man aged forty-two, with a battered and pugnacious face. He had joined the Royal Air Force during the early years of the service, seeing his first action in the Chanak Peninsula in Turkey. As a flight sergeant in the RAF Police, he had headed the nucleus of the newly formed Special Investigation Branch or 'SIB'. He was tenacious, perhaps unorthodox, but a skilled interrogator, with an unconcealed contempt for civilian detective procedures, particularly those of Scotland Yard.

Frank McKenna was considered too old to be a pilot. He was perhaps closer to the Stalag Luft 3 tragedy as he had known several officers who were held in Sagan, and two of them had been shot. Whilst sitting in a room full of aircrew, a BBC broadcast of Mr Eden's solemn words: *'His Majesty's Government... will never cease in their efforts to collect the evidence to identify all those responsible. They are firmly resolved that these foul*

---

[28] Allen Andrews, Exemplary Justice (London: Harrap 1976), p6.

criminals shall be tracked down to the last man, wherever they may take refuge. When the war is over they will be brought to exemplary justice.'

McKenna said to another former policeman—*'He doesn't know what he's talking about. Track them down to the last man, in war-busted Germany, when they'll have the best sets of false papers the Gestapo can provide!'* [29]

McKenna was well aware of the challenges that were facing any investigation; however, he could not foresee his future role as the lead investigator achieving the largest number of arrests of those responsible for the murders. Before Christmas 1944, McKenna was transferred to the Special Investigation Branch at Princes Gate Court, London, nearly eighteen months after some of the murders. McKenna flew to Germany to begin initial preparations. He spoke little German, but he was partnered with an investigator and interpreter, Warrant Officer H J Williams.

Flight Lieutenant Arthur R. Lyon was a tall, slim, pipe-smoking man, also twenty-eight, with a flair for languages. He had served as a station inspector in various Metropolitan divisions, including a year in the East End during the London blitz, before joining the Intelligence Service of the Royal Air Force. As a fluent German speaker, he was working in a unit interrogating captured members of the Luftwaffe who were thought to have specialised knowledge of new aircraft, armament, electronic equipment and tactics.

The full list[30] of officers involved in the murder enquiry:

Wing Commander Wilfred Bowes OBE (43664)

Squadron Leader Francis Peter McKenna OBE (2212815)

Squadron Leader William W P Thomas (Temporary attachment until McKenna was promoted to the rank of Squadron Leader)

Flight Lieutenant Arthur R Lyon (172337)

Flight Lieutenant Stephen H Courtney (197288)

Flight Lieutenant Harold E Harrison (197107)

Flying Officer David H Walker (Temporary attachment)

---

[29] Allen Andrews, Exemplary Justice (London: Harrap 1976), p34.
[30] Stephen R. Davies, A Global History of the RAF Police vol 5 (Kindle: 2012), p171.

*

On 1 July 1945, Wilfred Bowes was promoted to Squadron Leader. After this, he moved to Rinteln, a town in Lower Saxony, to command the SIB within the British Air Forces of Occupation. Bowes and his deputy Frank McKenna headed the 15-man investigation detachment, which was a small unit, and they very quickly realised it was insufficient for the immense task which faced them. This rather complex assignment to track down those responsible for the murders of fifty officers was never going to be easy. And they soon became aware of the many obstacles that would hinder their investigation.

One aspect of the case which caused them problems was the delay between when the crimes were committed and the start of their search. The investigation began seventeen months after the murders, making it a cold case. The investigators knew that the RAF men had been killed in various locations, but the SIB had only a small amount of reliable information to begin their investigation with. Eyewitnesses who had been held in jails alongside their murdered comrades provided what information they could, but this was only the basic details like dates and places where they were held—but crucially, none had witnessed the killings. Very quickly, the investigators realised that they were looking at several cold cases rather than just one.

More information was gained from the names of the places where the bodies were cremated, but those details were incomplete. Some of the urns returned to Sagan had no names, no location of the cremation, and often no date. The investigators were not looking for just a few suspects it was a much wider conspiracy. Each of the murders needed to be investigated in different former military districts of the Reich, and the biggest challenge was to find reliable sources of information in a war-shattered Germany to allow them to build cases against those who were guilty.

As investigators later found out, the perpetrators *'belonged to a body, the Secret State Police or Gestapo, which held and exercised every facility to provide its members with false identities and forged identification papers immediately after they were ordered to go on the run at the moment of national surrender.'* [31]

---

[31] Allen Andrews, Exemplary Justice (London: Harrap 1976), p7.

SECRET.   S18/1084/23

Officer Commanding, Special Investigation Branch, B.A.F.O.
Command Regiment Officer, B.A.F.O. (Ops) H.Q.

18th May 1946.
SIB/1084/45.

MURDER OF 50 R.A.F. OFFICERS - STALAG LUFT III.

In further reference to the conversation this morning between Wing Commander BOWES and Squadron Leader DEAN, it is requested that the necessary arrangements be made for the collection of 63 Germans presently detained in Camps in the American Zone of Occupation, and required in connexion with the enquiries and the subsequent trials in this case. It is desired that the convoy should leave your Headquarters for the American Zone on Thursday, 23rd May 1946.

2. Warrant Officer Williams of this Branch will accompany Flying Officer Newton of 2865 RAF Regiment Squadron, the Officer i/c the convoy, and will render any assistance necessary in the extradition of these germans. They will be transferred to Camp Number 101 ESTERWEGEN in the same manner as the previous 39 transferred by Number 2865 RAF Regiment Squadron, in April.

Wing Commander,
Commanding,
Special Investigation Branch,
B. A. F. O.

To highlight the scale of the investigation and the problems they faced, a confidential document in the archives headed 'Murder of 50 RAF Officers - Stalag Luft III' details the transfer request of 63 suspects being held in the American zone of Germany. The team faced not only a lack of cooperation from the Russians but also from the American authorities who at that time held many of the suspects wanted by the SIB for questioning.

Another secret memo sent between members of the investigation team and dated April 25, 1946, lists the names of SS officers the Americans refused to release from their custody. The file states: *'The following personnel cannot be handed over to the British authorities as they are required by the American authorities... they will be handed over when their usefulness to the Americans has been served.'* [32]

How were the investigation team going to be able to build prosecutions against those responsible if they were not able to interview potential witnesses or those whom they suspected of being involved?

Frank McKenna

Assigned to lead the investigation on the ground, Frank McKenna brought together a small, independent and dedicated team. Never larger than five officers and 14 NCOs it evolved into a copybook civilian detective investigation.

On 3 July 1945, McKenna was appointed Deputy Assistant Provost Marshal, and on 3 September he flew to Buckeburg, Germany to an airfield near Minden, west of Hannover to begin the immense challenge of finding those responsible for the murders of fifty RAF officers.

The initial stages of the investigation began on the ground, with investigators travelling to various places within the area of British control. Under the personal direction of the Provost Marshal of the RAF, enquiries were begun in cooperation with the Judge Advocate General's War Crimes Section, Military Intelligence, United States Army War Crimes Liaison and the Czech and French War Crimes Commissions. At a later stage in the investigation and with the consent of the Russian authorities, the former Gestapo chief in Breslau was interviewed in Moscow.

McKenna is recorded as being a man of impressive stature and an extremely effective interrogator. During the period of the investigation, he was promoted to squadron leader. Often, he led armed raids on those places where suspects wanted for investigation were thought to be living. The men who were wanted for questioning had false identities and often were living in plain sight. Even if their identities were suspected of being false, many still believed in what Nazi Germany had fought for and were reluctant to betray their comrades.

The team from the RAF relentlessly tracked down, arrested, and interrogated those they suspected were responsible for the murders or could provide information on the whereabouts of others. McKenna himself arrested more than twenty of the former

---

[32] AIR40/2488, Ancestry.com.

Gestapo officers, the largest single total out of the sixty-nine men brought to justice. Others committed suicide rather than face trial.

Once suspects were identified and arrested, they were interrogated. Those who were considered to be involved and perhaps guilty were transferred to England. They were then held at a facility known as the 'London Cage' and its interrogation methods were later called into question.

*

The SIB managed to locate various officials who had worked in offices within the Reich Security Main Office, the RSHA. One such individual, Peter Mohr was an inspector with the police and from 1943 worked in Berlin. From his testimony, the inspectors learned some of the details of how the search for those who'd escaped from Stalag Luft 3 was conducted and the decision-making behind the selection of those to be killed.

At the Nuremberg trials, the senior criminal police official in Breslau, Max Wielen gave evidence in a statement in which he stated the camp authorities were requested to compile a list of names and those who were regarded as disturbing elements and escape leaders were specifically mentioned. This list whilst put together either by the camp commandant von Lindeiner or one of his subordinates.

The RHSA was divided into several departments with various functions. Department V was the criminal police, the *Kriminalpolizei* or the 'Kripo', and Department IV was the secret state police, the *Geheime Staatspolizei* or the 'Gestapo'.

Once the list of names was received in Berlin, the shooting of officers mentioned by name was accordingly ordered by Department IV and corresponding instructions were sent to the Staatspolizei of the district concerned.

It is understood that SS-*Gruppenführer* Arthur Nebe, head of the *Kriminalpolizei* in Berlin, received the list of escapees from the camp and handpicked each of the men to be shot from their prison-of-war cards, copies of which were held in Berlin and at the camps where the men were held. Nebe made the selection, and this list was passed higher up the chain of command before being sent by secret message to the various Gestapo offices and they were instructed to carry out the executions. Once these were completed, a report was to be sent to Berlin.

*

The British government had learned of the deaths of the RAF officers from a routine visit in May 1944 to Stalag Luft 3 by the neutral Swiss authorities. Switzerland took over the role of protecting power from the United States after it had joined the war against Germany. The British Foreign Secretary Anthony Eden made an announcement to the House of Commons on 19 May 1944, after the British Government had received news of the murders.

Shortly after the announcement had been made the Senior British Officer at Stalag Luft 3, Group Captain Herbert Massey, was repatriated to England due to ill health. On 6 April, Massey was informed of the deaths of forty-one officers who had been shot and killed whilst trying to escape. Two days later, he was informed that he was going to be repatriated. After leaving the camp he learned from two medical orderlies that the number known to be killed was now forty-seven.

After his return, Massey was able to directly inform the Government of what he knew of the circumstances surrounding the escape and the almost certain murder of the recaptured prisoners. With this information, Eden updated Parliament on 23 June, promising that at the end of the war, those responsible would, in his words, be brought to 'exemplary justice'. This promise was repeated to the House a few weeks later.

23 June 1944

His Majesty's Government must, therefore, record their solemn protest against these cold-blooded acts of butchery. They will never cease in their efforts to collect the evidence to identify all those responsible. They are firmly resolved that these foul criminals shall be tracked down to the last man wherever they may take refuge. When the war is over they will be brought to exemplary justice. [33]

13 July 1944

His Majesty's Government's policy is that the foul criminals responsible for this cold-blooded act of butchery should be tracked down to the last man and brought to exemplary justice. It is our firm intention that all who are responsible for this crime, and all who have connived at it, whether they be military authorities or others, shall be pursued and brought to exemplary justice. And we shall make this clear to the German people by any and every means in our power, in order that they may be in no doubt as to what will be the fate of those, whoever they may be, whether they be high or low, who lend themselves, either as principals or agents, to the commission of these abominable crimes. [34]

---

[33] Anthony Eden. Hansard, 23 June 1944.
[34] Anthony Eden. Hansard, 13 July 1944.

West Prussia and Danzig

After the occupation of Poland in September 1939, the region known to the Germans as '*Reichsgau Danzig-Westpreußen*' was formed. It comprised most of the former Prussian province of West Prussia, including the 'Free City of Danzig', which before the September Campaign, was an open city although rather dominated by the German population.

The much-resented 'Polish Corridor' disappeared. This had been created as part of the agreements during the peace conference following the Great War. This corridor was never accepted by the German people and provided a reason for further conflict. The Great War had not been started by the Germans and they felt that they were unduly punished by the post-war settlements and massive reparations which they were required to pay the French.

This region had access to the sea from major ports such as Danzig, Elbing and Königsberg. Prisoners of war who escaped often aimed for these places in the hope of finding friendly passage to a neutral country such as Sweden.

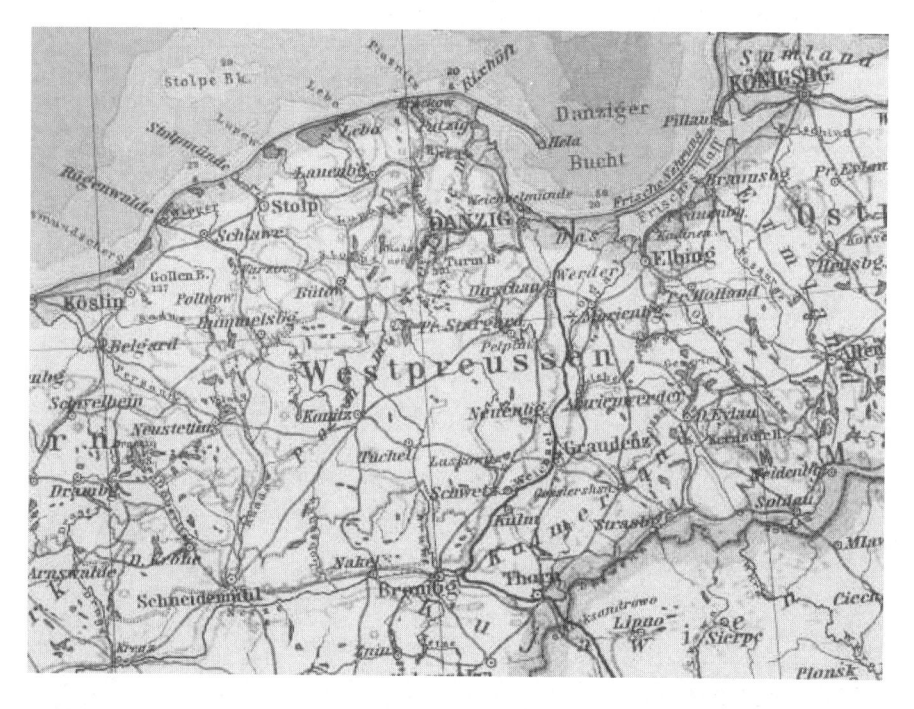

RAF Investigation – Early Days

The complex task which lay before the investigators was incredibly challenging, and there were many factors which hindered the investigation. A major problem was caused by the rapidly changing political climate in Europe with the defeat of Germany and this gave rise to increasing tensions between the Western Allies and the Soviet Union, an increasingly suspicious military ally. The RAF investigators had not only to deal with these political problems but also the lack of cooperation meant that they were not able to freely visit places in the Russian-controlled regions, such as Breslau and Danzig. These cities were effectively barred from the British by the post-war Soviet-controlled Polish authorities who were deeply suspicious of the purpose of the investigators.

Across Europe, the general focus was more on reconstruction and rebuilding rather than recriminations. The urgent needs of the many who had survived the war were of a higher priority than those who had perished. Restoring services, creating liveable cities and dealing with the huge number of displaced persons presented major challenges for European governments. Added to this, there were huge population shifts as German nationals were deported from areas like Upper and Lower Silesia, to be replaced with Poles from the former eastern Polish territories which were lost.

It was a daunting task for the investigators with all of the chaos in post-war Europe. Very little information relevant to the Sagan Case had emerged from interrogations which had been conducted in almost every camp in the British and American zones. The investigators had only uncovered a few of the former Danzig officials and too many of the most-wanted suspects were unaccounted for.

Of course, those who were in custody claimed to have little knowledge of the crimes during questioning, so they remained in custody and were held as potential witnesses.

One valuable source yielded suspects for the Danzig murders. Vital leads came from the interrogation of *Kriminaldirektor* Erich Graes, who had been deputy director of the *Kriminalpolitzei* or 'Kripo' in Danzig. At the end of the conflict, Graes was taken prisoner by the Americans and held for questioning.

Graes was a senior police official, and as such was responsible for searches and the recapture of escaped prisoners. Following the escape from Stalag Luft 3, the highest level of alert was raised known as the *Grossfahndung* or nationwide priority search. It had begun soon after the mass breakout from the camp had been discovered. Graes was in control of the search in the Danzig region. The SIB had discovered that

Walenn and his companions were recaptured shortly after the escape, however, the exact details were still something of a mystery.

The Nationwide Search—Grossfahndung

The German authorities were able to utilise various civilian and police units in searches, that could be instigated in increasingly higher levels. If required, these searches could involve all branches of the police augmented by civilians temporarily pressed into police service such as the Hitler Youth organisation.

The *Grossfahndung* was the highest level of search and was only used on exceptional occasions when it was deemed necessary, simply because it engaged large numbers of people in the search who were thus prevented from carrying out their normal responsibilities. The escape from Stalag Luft 3 in March was considered serious enough for just such a high level of alert to be ordered. Records show that this was perhaps only the second time that such an alert was issued.

Grossfahndung meant the mobilisation of all branches of the Police including all auxiliaries, Party Formations, Affiliated Organisations and whatever units of the Wehrmacht could be mustered, and this greatly interfered with almost every normal activity in Germany. To avoid this disruption an alert of this level was rarely issued, although more localised searches were much more frequent.

Allied POWs were not content with being held behind the wire and many of them were always looking for ways to regain their freedom.

*

During the investigation, the SIB conducted many thousands of formal interviews and spoke with all manner of people, both civilian and military. Some of the witnesses had held various positions within the police or military units of the defeated enemy. As such, they were often unfriendly or even hostile towards the investigators.

Those interviewed ranged from low-level officials to those who had held senior positions in the criminal police or the secret police. Perhaps these individuals were not necessarily directly involved with the killings or the Sagan Case, but they had at least performed some function within the military state which had facilitated mass murder. It was never going to be possible to prosecute everyone for their involvement, but clerks or drivers could provide valuable testimony that would be essential in piecing together prosecution cases against more senior officials suspected of committing crimes. These were the ones who were the most wanted suspects, those who either pulled the trigger or gave orders for others to do so. Those officials who were not involved directly with the Sagan murders may well have been guilty of other crimes and were therefore reluctant to cooperate. Most of them could never be described as innocent; many of the senior police officials had been in charge of death squads that had killed thousands if not tens of thousands.

Just before the 1941 Nazi invasion of the Soviet Union, the *Einsatzgruppen* or mobile death squads, which had previously operated in Poland, were placed once more under the overall command of Reinhard Heydrich.

Arthur Nebe volunteered to command *Einsatzgruppe* B, an SS death squad that operated behind Army Group Centre as the invasion into Russian territory progressed. The task of the *Einsatzgruppen* was to exterminate Jews and other 'undesirables' in territory overrun by the Wehrmacht. These were organised mass killing operations and men like Nebe led other SS officers in carrying out these murders.

Around 5 July 1941, Nebe led *Einsatzgruppe* B in the region of Minsk and remained there for two months. The murders progressed swiftly. In a 13 July Operational Situation Report, Nebe stated that 1,050 Jews had been killed in Minsk, also noting that the liquidations were underway in Vilna where around 500 men, women and children were shot daily. Nebe remarked: 'Only 96 Jews were executed in Grodno and Lida during the first days. I gave orders to intensify these activities.' He also added that the killings were being brought into smooth running order and shootings were carried out at 'an increasing rate.' The report also announced that his *Einsatzgruppe* was now killing non-Jews in Minsk.[35]

The former Gestapo chief of Breslau was sought by the investigation team for his involvement in the deaths of twenty-nine of the RAF officers. At the beginning of the German invasion of Poland, SS-*Sturmbannführer* Wilhelm Scharpwinkel had led *Einsatzkommando* 1/III, which was part of *Einsatzgruppe* III or EG III–Breslau (under SS-*Obersturmbannführer* and *Regierungsrat* Hans Fischer), these units were deployed with the 8th Army.

Another suspect wanted by the investigators was Günther Venediger, the former Gestapo chief in Danzig. In December 1939, he was appointed head of the Gestapo post in Grudziądz; his responsibilities there included the extermination and deportation of the Polish and Jewish population in that area. On 30 January 1940, he was promoted to SS-*Sturmbannführer*, and on 9 November 1943 to SS-

---

[35] Ronald Headland, Messages of Murder: A Study of the Reports of the Security Police and the Security Service (Fairleigh Dickinson, 1992).

Obersturmbannführer (lieutenant colonel). Despite his young age, in August 1941 he became the head of the important Gestapo office in Danzig.

Whether these men were guilty of involvement in the murders of the Sagan Case or not, they certainly had plenty of blood on their hands.

Recapture – how the investigation unfolded

Following the discovery of the escape attempt from Stalag Luft 3, the alert went out and the *Grossfahndung* began. This was on 25 March, the same day as the mass breakout. As the alert spread escapers encountered more patrols and increased scrutiny of their identity documents. Anyone who was considered suspicious or perhaps travelling without the correct documentation was taken to the nearest police station or military post. In this way, other escaped prisoners, forced labourers attempting to return to their homes, or deserters from the German military were also caught up in the search.

In his book, Allen Andrews gives the briefest of details as to the recapture of Walenn, Picard, Marcinkus and Brettell.

Flight Lieutenant Gilbert W. Walenn, Royal Air Force, was born in London 24th February 1916. Prisoner of war 11th September 1941. Headed the forgery department. Recaptured at Schneidemühl. Died 29th March 1944. Cremated at Danzig. [36]

The interrogation of *Kriminaldirektor* Erich Graes, the former deputy director of the criminal police in Danzig, had yielded the names of several persons who were wanted for questioning. He also gave information to the investigators of what he knew of the arrests.

Erich Graes

At the end of the war, Erich Graes was taken prisoner by the Americans and interned in a camp near Neumünster until at least 1947. At that time, the British military investigators were granted access to the prisoner and heard him as a witness in connection with the Sagan murders.

Graes joined the police in 1926 and held various positions during the early part of his career. In 1934 he was transferred to the German secret state police, the Gestapo, working in the department for Counterintelligence. In 1939, Graes was seconded to

---

[36] Allen Andrews, Exemplary Justice (London: Harrap 1976), p268.

Einsatzgruppe VI, as a representative of the task force in Posen. He later headed the establishment of the criminal police office in Posen, which he was busy with until his assignment ended on May 23, 1940.

On 14 June 1940, Graes applied for membership in the NSDAP[37] which was granted in July. Following this, Graes was transferred to the police administration in Magdeburg. More importantly, from April 1943 until the end of the war, Graes served as head of the criminal police control centre in Danzig. His immediate superior was the inspector of the security police and the SD Hellmut Willich.

At the time of The Great Escape, Graes was the deputy director of the *Kriminalpolizei* and he was responsible for organising the regional search—the *Grossfahndung*—in the Danzig military district.

Graes gave his statement to the investigators; four Royal Air Force officers had been taken off a train in the region of Danzig and held at Stalag XX B/Willenberg, a prisoner-of-war camp near Marienburg. From there, the criminal police transferred them to Danzig once their identities had been confirmed. Under guard, they were taken by truck, and the four officers were held in the police prison adjacent to the Gestapo office. Graes informed the head of the prison that the men were officers, that they should be kept in appropriate cells, and that they were to be treated well.

Walenn and the others arrived at the prison during the night. When Graes arrived at his office the next morning, he telephoned the head of the prison only to be informed that the men were no longer there, that they had been removed by the Gestapo. Graes could also recall that a top-secret teleprint message was received a few days later with orders to have the urns containing the ashes of the four officers taken to Breslau, to be handed over to the criminal police there.

Graes gave his British interrogators the names of two people who he felt were certain to know more about the details of the killings:

SS Standartenführer, Oberregierungsrat and Kommandeur der Sicherheitspolizei (SIPO) Günther Venediger; now thirty-eight years old; 1.82 m. high (almost six feet); dark hair; remarkable steel-blue eyes; a saddle nose; would certainly have false papers;

SS Brigade Führer, General-major der Polizei Helmut Willich; now aged fifty; height 1.74; greying brown hair; many wrinkles on face; alcoholic complexion; blue watery eyes with bags under them; walked with short steps; would certainly have false papers.

---

[37] National Socialist German Workers' Party (German: *Nationalsozialistische Deutsche Arbeiterpartei* or NSDAP.

Since the investigators had already discovered that the murders had been perpetrated by the Gestapo, they were confident that they now had the name of the man who was almost certainly responsible for orchestrating the killings. The head of Danzig Gestapo, Dr Günther Venediger.

Graes went on to tell the investigators that after the deaths of fifty officers had become international knowledge, he directly challenged Venediger about the deaths. He accused him of having the four officers shot in the Gestapo prison at Matzkaw.

Venediger merely replied, *'We don't do that sort of thing in Matzkaw'*.[38]

This was a rather evasive answer which could easily have meant that Venediger was fully aware of the circumstances of the murders and exactly where they had been committed—just that this had not taken place in Danzig-Matzkau[39].

*

Danzig-Matzkau was a police and SS prison camp near Danzig. It was subordinate to the Waffen-SS. This rehabilitation camp was primarily for Waffen-SS, particularly Officers and non-commissioned officers who had been charged with disciplinary infractions. It was set up using Polish forced labourers at the site of a former Polish Army camp. It was later transferred to the Waffen-SS, who reorganised it into a punishment camp for serious offenders within the ranks of Waffen-SS.

Graes — Court Testimony

When court proceedings against some of those responsible for the murders began in 1947 at the Curiohaus in Hamburg, the testimony of witnesses like Graes was essential to build the case for the prosecution.

He gave the following information in his testimony.

'In the spring of 1944, a number of English prisoners of war escaped from a prisoner of war camp in Germany, I remember the town of Sagan. There may have been around 80 prisoners.

Because of this escape, Berlin ordered a special large-scale manhunt throughout the Reich. Four English prisoners of war were arrested near Danzig. The English were handed over to the Gestapo by officers from the Danzig criminal police. WILLIG was informed of the arrest. On special orders from the security chief or directly from HIMMLER, the four English prisoners of war were shot near

---

[38] Allen Andrews, Exemplary Justice (London: Harrap 1976), p191.
[39] Strafvollzugslager der SS und Polizei in Danzig-Matzkau.

Danzig. No court proceedings took place. These were determined by the head of the Gestapo with the knowledge of Inspector WILLIG.' [40]

After the breakout from Sagan, a major manhunt was launched. Such large-scale manhunts, led by the war investigation centre of the Reich Criminal Police Office in Berlin, occurred frequently. There was a precise plan for this, based on which every department of the police, the Wehrmacht and other organizations knew which search measures had to be carried out in detail. Over a few days, most of the escaped flying officers were recaptured.

*

Graes was unclear on the specific details, but he knew that the men had been recaptured on a train in the Danzig area. The investigators knew that the men were last seen in Küstrin on 25 March, that they were travelling east, and that they were carrying false documents when recaptured.

The timeline suggests they were recaptured late in the afternoon or evening of 25 March. Following this, they were taken the same day to Marienburg, and sometime later transported from the Stalag to Danzig. After a few hours in the criminal police prison, they were taken away. If so, then what happened next?

---

[40] Archives of the Pilecki Institute. Warsaw. IP/Arch/7/35.8.10.2/758. Access date 23.11.2023. Creator's ref no: B162/27884. Bundesarchiv. Zentrale Stelle der Landesjustizverwaltungen zur Aufklärung nationalsozialistischer Verbrechen.

Kurt Achterberg

Flight Lieutenant Lyon interrogated Gestapo suspects at a camp in Esterwegen. When he was there, he gave some advice to a colleague.

He said, *The basic art of interrogation is to understand what is required and why it is required. The man who's being interrogated is usually holding something back. These Gestapo types are full of arrogance.'* [41]

Graes had also provided the name of a third suspect, who was also partly in the picture: SS *Sturmbannführer*, Regierungsrat Kurt Achterberg, who had been a deputy to Venediger.

Achterberg, now aged forty; height 1.80; wears glasses; very unruly brown hair brushed back; grey-blue eyes; rather unmilitary gait; big feet; big ears; lower lip underslung; bad teeth, yellow and irregular with some gold fillings. [42]

As the German defence on the Eastern Front collapsed, men like Achterberg fled westwards. He was not carrying false papers and was quickly caught. After over a year in the detention camp, he heard from other prisoners that there was an investigator conducting interrogations, so he voluntarily approached the Camp Registry saying that he could provide useful information. Achterberg was a tall, thin man with sharp features and eyes that flitted in all directions. Now Achterberg, without any of his previous arrogance, was given a private interview with Lyon.

Perhaps Achterberg was concerned about his situation, whether he was considered a suspect that could lead to possible prosecution and his death. He had always declared that he had known nothing about the Danzig murders but if he could give the investigators another name, then maybe that would divert their attention away from him onto someone else.

Rather pompously, he began *'I have been in conference with some of my colleagues from the Danzig Gestapo who are interned here, ...'*

Now with his memory prompted, he asked Lyon if he was aware of Günther Venediger, the Danzig Gestapo chief. Which of course, Lyon was.

---

[41] Alan Burgess The Longest Tunnel (London: Bloomsbury, 1990), p254.
[42] National Archives.

Did the Major know about criminal secretary Reinhold Bruchhardt, who was the hatchet man for special assignments in Danzig? This piqued Lyon's interest. Achterberg continued by saying that none of the Gestapo members interned at the camp were involved in the murders. As they had been at the camp for over a year, they reasoned that if they could help the inspectors with the enquiry, then the whole matter could be cleared up and they would be released.

Achterberg handed Lyon the address of Bruchhardt's wife, who was living at a place in the Hamburg area. As he passed over the address, he claimed that he and the other men knew nothing about the whereabouts of Dr Venediger.

Achterberg paused.

'I must give you a warning', he said. 'Bruchhardt was a terror. He has shot people in his office and in the street. He always had a rawhide whip soaking in a bucket of water by his desk, and he used this personally and often. Herr Hauptmann, if you do find Bruchhardt, for God's sake be careful. He is a dangerous man, and he is always armed. I advise you to shoot him dead if he flicks an eyelid.' [43]

*

Lyon knew that these former Gestapo men were now cowed, but perhaps he also sensed that they might be fighting for their lives. Almost none of them could consider themselves innocent, moreover, with their police backgrounds, they were rather accomplished at lies and deception.

Lyon and the investigation team had a lead on Frau Bruchhardt, perhaps she would be able to give them information about her husband. An armed unit was sent to the address, and they found an angry and vindictive wife who was happy to give the investigators another address, at a place called Kempten.

Separately McKenna had given up on interrogations at Neuengamme and had telephoned Esterwegen. He was informed about Achterberg, so he travelled to the camp to speak with him. McKenna asked about Bruchhardt, and when he saw Achterberg's reaction he knew there was something there. Achterberg admitted to knowing Bruchhardt and that he disliked the man. He confessed the reason for this, Bruchhardt was having an affair with his wife. Then he gave McKenna the address of a woman in Kempten who may be able to help, and this matched the address previously given to Lyon by Bruchhardt's wife.

---

[43] Allen Andrews, Exemplary Justice (London: Harrap 1976), p192.

Men were dispatched to the address. The woman was named Frau Blum and although she was initially reluctant, she gave the investigators another address and also the name that Bruchhardt was using at that time. With this new lead, both McKenna and Lyon led an armed squad to follow it up and as they entered the flat, they found their man asleep in bed. He awoke with a start, instinctively reaching for a pistol which he had near the bed. Bruchhardt was an enormous man and was only subdued after a struggle with the armed officers.

McKenna was now convinced they had got their man.

Achterberg was the source of the information about Bruchhardt and yet obviously he was neither impartial nor unbiased towards him. His willingness to offer up Bruchhardt as the main suspect in the murders of the Danzig group was perhaps treated with a little scepticism. Lyon knew that these men had been Gestapo officials and that they were accomplished liars—perhaps Achterberg was not just trying to save his own skin, maybe he was also trying to get revenge on the man who was having an affair with his wife.

Stalag XX B / Willenberg

As their train rolled into the station, the four men prepared themselves before they stepped down onto the platform. Walenn surely felt a moment of satisfaction as the guard studied his papers and allowed him to continue without hindrance. The dishevelled appearance of the four men and their French peasant clothing aroused no suspicions; their excellently forged documentation identified them as foreign workers, which is what they appeared to be.

As they made their way out of the station perhaps the four men exchanged glances and talked quickly about what they should do next. Whether to continue their journey or maybe to find someplace to sleep for a few hours? They would have decided quickly to avoid arousing any suspicions. To travel further east they needed to cross a bridge over the river Weichsel, now called the Vistula, which presented a formidable obstacle to their onward progress.

At Dirschau, there was a major rail bridge and a separate bridge for road traffic. Although these bridges had been damaged during the invasion of Poland in the September campaign, pedestrians had access to the bridges which would have allowed the group of four to cross over the otherwise impassable river. This late in the day, the men knew that their absence from Stalag Luft 3 would have been discovered, but how quickly could a warning go out to all of the police units across German-controlled territory? As the four had already gone through many checkpoints to reach this stage of their journey, perhaps they felt their luck would hold. However, in the town or on the bridge the men were challenged at a checkpoint. Something went wrong for them, and the four quickly found themselves being escorted under guard by a unit of the Wehrmacht to Stalag XX B/Willenberg.

Later the following day, Walenn lay on the paillasse and wooden bed, weary after everything which had occurred over the last few days. His mind raced; would they be able to get away somehow? He'd discussed the possibility of escape with the warrant officer in charge of the clothing store at the camp. The platoon sergeant major had been suspicious at first, unsure whether he should trust them, but he had agreed to speak to someone in charge of escapes. Maybe they could do something to help.

*

The RAF investigators probed into the personalities of Stalag XX B/Willenberg, which was about 60 miles south of Danzig, just east of Dirschau. In the summer of 1945, this yielded a statement from Company Sergeant-Major J. Fulton of the 2nd Seaforth Highlanders, who had been British Man of Confidence—the senior ranking man at this camp. He remembered that he returned with a working party on an evening at the end of March 1944, and heard that four RAF officers, who had been put into sharp arrest on the previous night, had been taken away.

Another witness, Platoon Serjeant Major Albert Hicks was the warrant officer in charge of Red Cross clothing at the camp. Hicks was a Platoon Sergeant Major of the Wiltshire Regiment, which had been part of the British Expeditionary Force (BEF) in France before the German invasion in the spring of 1940. Hicks had been captured in June and was held at Stalag XX B.

On the morning of Sunday 26th March, fellow POW Corporal Becker brought Hicks a message to say that four British officers had arrived in the camp and he asked Hicks to provide clothing for the group. Entering the clothing store, he found the four men in what appeared to be civilian clothing, and their spokesman began to enquire about any escape club within the camp.

Although Hicks was initially wary, the spokesman offered proof of who he was, in the form of his identity disc. From memory, Hicks described the spokesman as having a bushy, black moustache and an English accent. Appearing to be about 30 to 40 years of age although this was difficult to tell for sure. Once convinced that the men were indeed escaped British officers, Hicks confirmed that there was an escape club and that they would do everything in their power to help the Englishman and his companions.

To start with, Hicks issued the four men with more appropriate military clothing which included khaki battledress and other items and the four dispensed with their less-than-regulation clothing. With foresight, he did not issue them overcoats or blankets, thereby giving him a pretext to find out later which cell the men were being kept in. Knowledge of the men's location would be useful for the escape organisation.

The spokesman for the group gave the impression of being a senior officer, and he also impressed upon Hicks the urgency of the situation, and that they must re-escape that night. After leaving the clothing store, Hicks made contact with company sergeant major A. Dean of the Field Security Police who oversaw everything connected to escape attempts.

After approximately half an hour, Hicks persuaded the Germans to allow him to take overcoats and blankets to the officers in their cells. Hicks returned to where the four were being kept in individual cells and separate from the other prisoners, carrying khaki greatcoats and blankets for them. He talked his way past the guards and distributed the coats amongst the four, noting at the same time which cells they were being held in. Each of the four cells was guarded by an officer, and there were two more guarding the block.

The men were being held separately, but after verifying the cell numbers and their locations, Hicks took the information to Dean, who in turn got to work trying to put together a plan to free the four airmen. With little time, a hasty plan to switch the men with other POWs was put together. Four substitutes were to take the places of the men in the cells. However, as the prisoners were closely watched by six guards, it proved far too difficult to make the switch. Walenn's group were taken away in a vehicle that same evening.

After the war, in a debriefing, he gave his witness statement. Hicks was unable to recall the names of the men and had not obtained their details for the Red Cross book. However, he said the men were all heavily bearded and dirty, and the spokesman had a bushy, black moustache and an English accent, which appears to be a fair description of Walenn. Hicks also remembered that the spokesman mentioned one of his fellow officers was Belgian, presumably Picard.

Albert Hicks was certain that it was a Sunday, maybe this had stuck in his mind because he'd attended a church service earlier that day. Although he did not witness the four men being taken away from the camp, he was told of this by a fellow POW whom he trusted, D.S.M. A. Dean.

*

When Hicks gave his statement to the investigating officers, he could recall the four men telling him that they had been caught in the neighbourhood of Dirschau, where there is a bridge over the Weichsel on the road connecting Marienburg with Danzig. Later, in his court statement, Hicks described the four officers as all heavily bearded and dirty, dressed in rough civilian clothing of the French peasant type. One of them had a French beret on. Importantly, Hicks stated that the men had told him where they had been recaptured—in the vicinity of Dirschau.

*

At the time, Dirschau was an important hub on the railway network. Trains ran through the city from the west and headed either north to Danzig or they crossed eastwards to Marienburg, the port city of Elbing, or Königsberg further along the Baltic coast. There was an important railway bridge across the river Weischel that had been damaged earlier in the war but at the time of the escape, it was a vital crossing point. Even today there are extensive railyards as the city is an important railway hub, no longer called Dirschau but Tczew, in Poland.

Where was Walenn's group recaptured?

> F/Lts. WALEN, MARCINKUS and BRETTELL and F/O. PICARD.
>
> On 26th March 1944 these officers were taken, after recapture, to Stalag XXB at Willenberg, where they were fitted out with army battledress. On the afternoon of that day they were seen leaving in a car escorted by armed N.C.Os of the camp staff whose instructions were to hand them over to the Gestapo at Danzig. The urns later received at the Stalag bore their names and show them to have been cremated at Danzig on a date unspecified.

The last information about these men from their brother officers. [44]

As Henri Picard was Belgian, it was thought by other escapers that he would most likely aim for that country with his escape partner Gordon Brettell. It is now impossible to know for sure, but maybe the pair had decided it was better to stay with Tim Walenn and Romas Marcinkus and make for Lithuania—the adage of safety in numbers.

From Küstrin, it would have been a long and difficult journey across Germany to reach Belgium—crossing Poland to Lithuania was a shorter distance with perhaps better chances of being aided by Polish civilians or the Polish Home Army. Whatever their reasoning, it is clear that the four remained together until the end.

One possible route the men aimed to follow was an express train to Frankfurt-an-der-Oder, a slow train to Küstrin, and an express train to Dirschau, just south of Danzig. Perhaps then with a final connection to the port of Danzig or the nearby port of Elbing.[45]

Somewhat confusingly, a report from a Swiss representative of The Swiss Protecting Power had reported privately to the British Government that, unknown to any German officials, Brettell, Marcinkus, Picard and Walenn had passed the night of 26th-27th March at Willenberg and the night of 27th-28th March in Danzig with work detachments from the British prisoner-of-war camp Stalag XX B.

Now more commonly referred to as Stalag XX B Marienburg, the Stalag was originally known at the time as XX B/Willenberg. This makes part of the Swiss report correct, the men were in the Stalag on 26 March, and late in the day, they were transferred to Danzig.

---

[44] IMT Nuremberg Archives H-1509

[45] Oliver Philpott, Stolen Journey (London: Hodder & Stoughton 1950), P282.

The rest of the report may simply have been misinformation from the German authorities. Fortunately for the investigators, they discovered reliable witnesses who had contact with the four officers.

Entrance to Stalag XX B/Willenberg, 1940. [46]

*

At the beginning of 1944, Stalag XX B held nearly 30,000 men POWs of various nationalities. Almost 10,000 British and French; nearly 5,000 Soviet and Italians. Together with men from Belgium, Poland, and Serbia. It may well be that when Walenn and his companions were arrested, they were taken by the Wehrmacht patrol to Stalag XX B on the assumption that they had escaped from there.

Walenn would have been confident of the documentation that the men possessed however military and police units were on high alert for suspicious-looking military-

---

[46] ICRC Audiovisual Archives.

aged men given that they may be either be escaped POWs or members of the Home Army—the Polish resistance organisation.

One thing is certain, Walenn, Picard, Marcinkus and Brettell travelled further than most of the other escapers. Marcinkus was Lithuanian, when they were recaptured, the group was approximately 300 km short of reaching his hometown. Most likely, the group had intended to travel to East Prussia and cross the Lithuanian border. Their escape plan was kept secret from other prisoners for security reasons, but it seems likely they were heading in the direction of Lithuania.

By leaving the train at Dirschau and avoiding the highly garrisoned city of Danzig, maybe Marcinkus and his colleagues felt they could find contacts who could help them cross the Baltic Sea to the safety of neutral Sweden.

Recaptured Near Dirschau

In the book *Exemplary Justice* by Allen Andrews, the author states that the *'four Royal Air Force officers had been taken off a train at Schneidemühl and put in a prisoner-of-war camp at Marienburg. Graes had them brought in by truck to Danzig and lodged in the police prison.'* [47]

Presumably, the source of this information was the statement taken from Erich Graes the former head of the *Kriminalpolizei* or 'Kripo' in Danzig. What appears strange, is that if the four men had been discovered on a train passing through Schneidemühl, why were they then taken on such a long journey further east?

Graes oversaw the *Grossfahndung* in the Danzig region, but the standard police procedure for dealing with suspicious persons was to transport them to the nearest police station or military post for questioning and to confirm their identities. This procedure was followed by police and Wehrmacht units, so was an exception made in this instance? Why were they taken so far from Sagan?

Following the procedure, the four men should have been taken to a regional Gestapo office or a prison-of-war camp closer to where they were recaptured. Along the train line from Schneidemühl were the towns of Neu-Bentschen, Woldenberg, and Flatow—all three had Gestapo offices. The third, Flatow, lay 33 km east of Schneidemühl. Added to that, there were prisoner-of-war camps at Thorn, Posen and Bromberg to which these men could have been taken until their identities were confirmed. It simply makes no sense that they were transferred so far east to Stalag XX B in Marienburg.

Graes would have been well aware that Schneidemühl lay outside of his area of responsibility. The territory controlled by the Third Reich was divided into military districts, which were created before the start of the war and existed until the final surrender of German forces. These districts are also known by their German name *Wehrkreise* (or the singular *Wehrkreis*). Schneidemühl was in a different *Wehrkreis* to Stalag XX B Marienburg and Stalag XX A Thorn, both of these camps were in the district *Wehrkreis* XX as indicated by the name, with Thorn being considerably closer to where the men were supposed to have been recaptured.

As Schneidemühl was in *Wehrkreis* II, this would have meant that any arrest in that city fell outside the jurisdiction of the Danzig police. If these airmen had been recaptured by officers from District II, then they would have been taken to the nearest police station or military command centre and not over the border into a neighbouring

---

[47] Allen Andrews, Exemplary Justice (London: Harrap 1976), p146.

district and certainly not on such a long journey of over two hundred kilometres further to the east. Whatever the case, the accepted story of the four men being recaptured in or near Schneidemühl seems inconsistent with the other arrests and this version of events simply doesn't add up.

German Districts - Wehrkreise

[Map showing German districts II and XX, with cities including Stolp, Kolberg, Danzig, Elbing, Konitz, Marienwerder, Schneidemühl, Bromberg, Thorn, Leslau, and Posen]

Kurt Lundehn's Testimony

During the trial in Hamburg, one of the men called as a witness was Kurt Ernst Lundehn. This officer had been conscripted into the Danzig Gestapo in 1940 and held no special rank. The witness confirmed that the Gestapo chief was indeed Günther Venediger and that he'd had that position for several years prior.

Lundehn also confirmed that in 1944, he was working within the Danzig Gestapo for Department III and took part in the search for the escaped airmen. He was made aware that 40-50 British officers had escaped and that was why a nationwide search was in effect. Lundehn, together with all of the Gestapo officials, was seconded to the Kripo for the search, and his particular role was to check the trains travelling between

Danzig, Konitz and Dirschau. Logically, when searches were performed the available manpower was focused on key areas, such as bridges which were key crossing points, and these could be guarded. Not every train station would need to be staffed with Gestapo officers, they could more easily focus on key junctions, such as Posen, Bromberg or Thorn where key railway lines intersected. Dirschau was such a station— linking the east-west line with that to Danzig further north.

In his court testimony, Lundehn stated that he never made any arrests and also did not hear of any such arrests in his area of search. This may not be that surprising given that almost two hundred men worked in the Gestapo at that time, plus other units such as the Kripo and Volkssturm[48], however, it also suggests the possibility that Walenn and his companions were not caught whilst travelling on a train.

*

Where the four airmen were recaptured is hard to confirm. German officials such as Graes and Lundehn, gave their statements to investigators but as they were not directly involved with the arrests they were uncertain of the specific details. The consensus is that the men were recaptured on a train, but whether the escapers were caught on a train, at a train station, or attempting to cross the bridge on their journey eastwards we may never know.

Graes oversaw the search in the Danzig area, he was not directly involved in the arrest of these men, however, Graes did confirm in his statement that the men were recaptured in the Danzig administration district either in or near Konitz and not Schneidemühl as is widely believed.

Weighing Graes's testimony against the affidavit produced in court by Albert Hicks, Platoon Serjeant Major of the Wiltshire Regiment, who clearly remembered having contact with the four officers on Sunday 26 March, then we should give more weight to this witness. From their testimonies, it is possible to deduce the timeline of events.

---

[48] A forced national militia established by Nazi germany in the closing stages of the WWII.

Neugarten 27, Danzig Gestapo

In the early hours of 27 March, the four prisoners were ordered to get ready to be transferred. They had only been in the Gestapo cells for a few hours and now they were being moved again. Feeling sleepy and weary, they rose from their beds and got ready as quickly as they could. With only a small bundle of clothing and a briefcase with them, this did not take long. They assembled in the corridor before being escorted up the stairs to where two vehicles were waiting.

A six-seater Mercedes was standing with the engine idling as the men were put into the back of the truck under armed guard. Even if they could there was nowhere to run to now as they were surrounded by the walls of the prison. As the gates opened, the first vehicle drove through, a four-door Hannomag carrying four men inside. The Mercedes truck followed and the vehicles turned right in the direction of the main road out of the city. As the four RAF officers sat on the benches in the back of the truck, perhaps they thought about how long the journey back to Sagan would take them—if that was their destination.

After approximately thirty minutes, the two vehicles came to a halt by the side of the road. It was still only about five in the morning so there was no other traffic about. The guards lowered the tailgate and ordered the men to get out. An officer from the first car came over and told the men that they were to relieve themselves now, as it would be a long journey.

The four RAF officers walked along a dirt track a short distance into the woods flanked by their armed escort. After just a few minutes, the men were told to halt. A short time later each of them lay dead.

*

The four RAF officers were moved from Stalag XX B on Sunday 26 March and killed on the following day. The bodies were taken to Gestapo HQ before transport to the crematorium. The date of 29 March which is marked on their headstones is the date on which the urns were collected from the crematorium.

RAF Investigation Progresses

Arrest of Reinhold Bruchhardt

Investigators from the SIB knew where to find Bruchhardt, they had been given an address. When they arrived at that address, they realised it was that of a police station. Initially, they thought they had been lied to, but soon they realised there were also residential flats above.

Inspector Lyon enquired if anyone lived at 22 Rathausstrasse. They awoke the concierge to get into the flats. The door was opened unlocked quietly and McKenna went inside wary of what he might find.

Someone was sitting bolt upright in bed. As McKenna turned on the lights the person lept out of bed and towards a corner cupboard. He was of a huge build, much the same as Achterberg. One of the officers looked inside the small cupboard and discovered a revolver. In the light, McKenna knew that they had found their man, so they got him to dress before taking him to the local prison.

The following morning, Bruchhardt was transferred to Minden which was a two-day journey by car. All the time he was under the watchful eye of Lyon who was armed. Bruchhardt was put into the holding prison at Minden.

The next day McKenna entered Bruchhardt's cell, to hear what the man had to say, and was shocked to find that Bruchhardt's eyes were almost completely closed and there was a gash and heavy bruising on his face.

McKenna asked what had happened.

Bruchardt said, 'You should know. You're in charge.' McKenna went outside and began questioning. He learned that the second-in-command of the military gaol, a warrant officer with a leaning towards alcohol, had come in late at night, scanned the register for new entries, found that someone was entered in connection with the Stalag Luft III murders, and gone into Bruchardt's cell and beaten him up single-handed. [49]

McKenna was disappointed. Bruchhardt refused to make any confession, and when he did make a statement he claimed that the murder of the four officers had been carried out by a special group of Ukrainians who had been employed in Danzig for terroristic action against partisan units. Unfortunately, there were no other witnesses.

The SIB knew the name of the senior Gestapo official in Danzig, but the whereabouts of Günther Venediger still eluded the investigation team. It was not known whether he was alive or dead. If he was alive, then it was almost certain that he had not passed through any of the interrogation centres within West Germany.

For the SIB, this was deeply frustrating, such a high-ranking official who had directed the murders of four RAF officers was still beyond the reach of British justice.

Gestapo Headquarters

After the truck had returned to Danzig, the personal possessions of each of the murdered airmen were brought to Bruchhardt's office. Personal items of each of the men were inside envelopes. Sorting through, Bruchhardt made a list of these items, such as watches, rings, and identity documents.

Each of the men also had carried with them a small suitcase containing clothing and laundry items, together with some tinned food.

Additionally, each man had carried a bundle of clothing. These were the roughly fashioned civilian clothing that the men had worn during their train journeys from Sagan. They had been made from military uniforms which had been altered and died black or blue. It was this clothing that had appeared to be civilian clothing of the French peasant type, that Warrant Officer Hicks had seen at Stalag XX B.

Bruchhardt labelled each bundle and suitcase with the names of the murdered men. Once this had been done, he went to speak with Venediger about the burial arrangements. It was then that Venediger informed him the bodies were to be cremated, ostensibly so that the ashes could be returned via the Red Cross. As this was not the normal procedure, both men were unsure as to what was required and Bruchhardt was told to contact the Danzig-Langfuhr crematorium.

---

[49] Allen Andrews, Exemplary Justice (London: Harrap 1976), p198.

As Bruchhardt was informing the Registry Office and obtaining the death certificates, back in the Gestapo yard the four bodies were placed inside coffins. The truck then delivered these coffins to the crematorium. After two days the urns were ready for collection.

The conspiracy of silence

Some weeks after the events in the forest, Bruchhardt was summoned with Hug and Sasse to see Venediger, who seemed a little concerned. The Gestapo chief informed the officers that the incident in connection with the shooting of prisoners of war had caused unpleasant echoes in Great Britain and certain other countries. He had been afraid of this and now felt that it may be necessary to permit an International Red Cross Commission to visit the scene of the incident. Clearly, it would be necessary to convince them that things had happened as expressed in the report. It was during this meeting that Venediger then asked his subordinates whether they would be prepared to appear as if they had been in charge of the prisoner escort—Bruchhardt as the senior officer, with Hug and Sasse as escorts.

Bruchhardt was surprised by this, and when Venediger noticed this, he pointed out that the Fatherland was in a battle for its life and death. Germany's enemies would try to damage its reputation in any way possible, furthermore, German prisoners were at risk of reprisals. It was of the utmost importance for Bruchhardt to create the right impression with the International Red Cross Commission and those who were responsible could not be entrusted with this responsibility.

Of course, Bruchhardt agreed to this because of his oaths of service and out of a sense of duty to the Führer and the Fatherland.

Meeting with Heinrich Müller

Bruchhardt was at the time convinced that the four officers had tried to escape and wrote the necessary report which detailed the events of what he believed to have transpired in the forest near Groß Trampken.

Other than visiting the scene on the morning of the murders, Venediger kept his involvement in the crime at a distance. Although Achterberg was his deputy, he ordered Bruchhardt to act as a courier and take the report to Berlin. As ordered, Bruchhardt travelled to the capital.

In September 1939, when the Gestapo and other police organizations were consolidated under Heydrich into the Reich Security Main Office (RSHA), Müller was made chief of the RSHA 'Amt IV' more commonly known as the Gestapo.

Bruchhardt met with Müller at the criminal police headquarters in Berlin. As he was pressed for time, Müller did not open the report but handed Bruchhardt a receipt for it. Bruchhardt was then dismissed.

Throughout the whole affair, Venediger gave the orders and directed the men under his command. He arranged for the transport of the prisoners, their murder, and the subsequent cover-up. As the senior Gestapo official in Danzig, it is without doubt that he was responsible for everything that occurred under his jurisdiction.

However, Venediger admitted later, that he was not present when the murders were carried out. If Bruchhardt's claim was correct, then Venediger also asked for his subordinate to falsify the report saying that it was under his supervision the squad had conducted the killings.

Did the Gestapo Chief Venediger also order someone to commit the crime before sending Bruchhardt to investigate?

MOHR dealt with the boxes which arrived in Berlin

During the court proceedings in 1947, Peter Mohr was asked about boxes. He recollected that the senior government councillor Dr Schultze had come from a conference with Heinrich Himmler and that he had brought with him two large-sized parcels which he then handed over to Mohr to examine and catalogue the contents, and to write out lists for those items.

Now in charge of these boxes, Mohr opened them and found the personal belongings of the murdered officers. Items such as watches, wallets, pictures, false personal documents, and rings. These were together with written interrogations that had been conducted by the Gestapo. Mohr quickly read through a few of the statements, realising that they all followed the same format and the officers had given only name, rank and number with no information about the escape to the interrogators.

Later, the boxes were dispatched to Breslau with instructions for Wielen to have them transported to Sagan. Sometime later, Mohr received a receipt from Sagan.

Curiously, the personal effects of the four RAF officers who had been murdered near Danzig were missing. After enquiring with Müller's adjutant, Mohr was informed that a big wooden case was being sent from the Gestapo office in Danzig. When it arrived, Mohr's presence was requested when it was opened. He could see that it contained envelopes, which were as described by Bruchhardt in his testimony. Not only did it contain the personal belongings of the dead men, but also all of their clothing and uniforms which they had carried with them.

Schulze asked Mohr to check to see if these uniforms had any traces of blood on them, which apparently, they did not. After a short time, Mohr was ordered to look after the personal items and leave the uniforms for disposal by the Gestapo.

The London Cage

Its commanding officer, Colonel Scotland, set the cage rules; and this is where the controversy emerged. At the end of the war, he faced repeated allegations from German prisoners of mistreatment and even torture. And all this just a stone's throw from Kensington Palace. [50]

Kensington Palace Gardens is one of the most exclusive, and expensive, addresses in the world: its stately row of 160-year-old mansions, built on land owned by the crown, is home to ambassadors, billionaires and princes.

Between July 1940 and September 1948, three of these magnificent houses were home to one of the country's most secret military establishments: the London office of the Combined Services Detailed Interrogation Centre, known colloquially as the 'London Cage'. The facility was run by MI19, the section of the War Office responsible for gathering information from enemy prisoners of war, and few outside this organisation knew exactly what went on beyond the single barbed-wire fence that separated the three houses from the busy streets and grand parks of west London.

Alexander Paterson Scotland

Alexander Paterson Scotland OBE (1882–1965) was a British Army officer and intelligence officer, who is most noted for his work during and after World War II when he was commander of the London Cage. A forceful, outspoken man he was considered to have the perfect background—although English, the colonel had served briefly in the German army. In 1939, at the age of 57, Scotland was recalled for service.

The London Cage had space for sixty prisoners at any time and five interrogation rooms. Scotland had around ten officers serving under him, plus a dozen NCOs who served as interrogators and interpreters.

The Secrets of the London Cage

Within the National Archives are documents from two official inquiries into the methods employed at the Cage, one which heard evidence that guards were under orders to knock on cell doors of certain prisoners every 15 minutes, depriving them

---

[50] Helen Fry, London Cage: The Secret History of Britain's World War II Interrogation Centre (Yale University Press, 2017), p 119.

of sleep, and another which concluded with 'the possibility that violence was used' during interrogations.

Similar torture allegations surfaced in 1947, and again the following year, during the Sagan trials. The court in Hamburg was told that many of the defendants had been starved and systematically beaten at the London Cage and threatened with electrical devices.

Erich Zacharias was one of the defendants at the first Sagan Trial. He had been a sergeant in the Gestapo's frontier police. The only evidence against him was his confession which, MI5 noted in its assessment of Scotland's memoir, had been signed only because 'being a prisoner in their hands, he had been worked on psychologically'. Zacharias insisted that he had also been beaten. Twenty of the defendants at the first trial were convicted and thirteen were hanged, Zacharias among them.

Was Scotland regarded as a maverick whose methods were to be quietly overlooked, or whether he was acting official approval is not clear. By late 1946, there was concern about his methods being expressed at the headquarters of the British army of the Rhine.

There is a long and detailed letter of complaint from one SS captain, Fritz Knoechlein, who described his treatment after being taken to the Cage in October 1946. Knoechlein alleged that because he was 'unable to make the desired confession.' He was stripped, given only a pair of pyjama trousers, and deprived of sleep and food for four days and nights.

As the work of the Cage was wound down, the interrogation of prisoners was switched to several of the internment camps in Germany. Exactly what kind of treatment men like Erich Zacharias, Johannes Post or Reinhold Bruchhardt suffered has not been recorded.

After Bruchhardt had been tracked down and arrested, following initial interrogations Wing Commander Bowes arranged for him to be transferred to the London Cage. The escorting guards were given a message for Colonel Scotland that Bruchhardt was highly dangerous. By the time he arrived, the investigation team had already reconstructed what they considered to be the part that Bruchhardt had played in the killings.

According to the court proceedings, the precise date of Bruchhardt's arrival at the London Cage was 22 July 1946. During the twenty-seven months he was held in England, he spent twenty-five of those in solitary confinement. At one point, he had been determined to prove his innocence and in his room at the cage, Bruchhardt readily began to write down his version of events. Scotland was unimpressed and told him that he did not believe a word. He told him straight: *'We know you were the man in charge of the special duty squad. You, and you only, were responsible for the murders. We already have all the evidence we want.'* [51]

Bruchhardt was kept under constant observation and kept occupied by scrubbing floors. He was later transferred from the cage and transferred to a prisoner-of-war camp in Colchester, where security was not as strict as at the London Cage.

One night, during Bruchhardt's incarceration there, he escaped over the boundary wall with another prisoner. They succeeded in living for three weeks undetected in woods near Colchester, raiding farms for food. Eventually, they were both arrested by police and transferred back to the London Cage. To prevent another escape, Bruchhardt was transferred to a prison in Sheffield while the war crimes case was prepared against him.

Then, in October 1948, he spent a brief time back at the London Cage before being transferred to Hamburg for the second Sagan trial which took place that same month.

During Bruchhardt's stay in the London Cage, Scotland was convinced that he had the man responsible for the shootings of the four RAF officers near Danzig. That the prisoner was a brutal killer is not in any doubt, but was he guilty of carrying out the murders of Walenn and the others in the forest near Danzig?

---

[51] Helen Fry, London Cage: The Secret History of Britain's World War II Interrogation Centre (Yale University Press, 2017), p 223.

Curiohaus Trials in Hamburg

After Germany was defeated, punishing those responsible for crimes committed by the leading Nazis, the German military, and members of the police units was an important post-war aim of the Allies. The Nuremberg Trials of the Major War Criminals attracted attention all over the world and is regarded as a milestone in legal history. However, what is far less well-known is that the Allies also conducted hundreds of other trials.

After the war, the British Army chose the Curiohaus building in Hamburg to hold these trials as it had not been damaged during the conflict. From 1945 to 1949, the most important court for trying war crimes in the British Zone was held in the Curiohaus. In total, 188 military trials against 504 defendants took place there. Proceedings were against former concentration camp officials, members of the security police, and other functionaries who were suspected of illegal killings.

*

On 3 May 1945, British troops entered the city of Hamburg, which surrendered without a fight. In front of the city hall, Major General Alwin Wolz handed over the city to the British Brigadier John Spurling. Spurling concentrated on ensuring the safety of the general public and providing food for the city's inhabitants. Another priority was the search and round-up of high-ranking Nazis. The former head of the Nazi party in Hamburg Gauleiter Kaufmann was arrested on 4 May 1945, followed by other members of the Nazi party and the SS.

On 10 May, Colonel Hugh Armytage began to establish the British Military Government in Hamburg. The crimes committed by the Germans during the war were truly horrific and the Allies were faced with an unprecedented situation. How were the Allies supposed to bring those responsible for the vast number of terrible Nazi crimes to justice?

In the London Charter issued on 8 August 1945, the British, American, French and Soviet governments agreed to establish an international military tribunal where the main German war criminals would stand trial, all following the rule of law. Other defendants would be tried in those countries where they had committed their crimes during German occupation.

In the British occupation zone of Germany, regulations for the punishment of violations of international law were established by a Royal Warrant. British military courts tried only war crimes committed against citizens of the Allied countries.

The Hamburg Trials – Sagan Case

The first trial relating to the Sagan Case took place in the period from 11 July to 3 September 1947. Max Wielen, the former head of the criminal police in Breslau, and seventeen Gestapo officials stood trial for their planning and involvement in the murders of the fifty British officers.

All the accused pleaded not guilty.

The verdicts and sentences were handed down after a full fifty days on 3 September of that year. Except for Wielen, the court accused all of them of having been personally involved in the killings.

Wielen had previously been called as a witness during the Nuremberg War Trials because of his knowledge of the Nazi High Command and their connection to the murder conspiracy. As head of the criminal police in Breslau, he had played a decisive role in the planning and cover-up of a majority of those murders. He was found guilty and sentenced to a life-long prison term for his involvement.

The other defendants at the trial were found not guilty of the first two charges, but guilty of individual charges of murder. Thirteen prisoners were sentenced to death, and they were hanged at Hameln Prison in February 1948.

The Second Sagan Trial

The second trial for the Sagan Case began in August 1948. Three men stood accused of murder—Erwin Wieczorek, Richard Hänsel and Reinhold Bruchhardt.

Wieczorek was tried for his role in the deaths of four airmen taken from Hirschberg prison and murdered on 29 March. He was also charged together with Hänsel for the deaths of six officers taken from Görlitz on 31 March.

Bruchhardt was charged alone with committing a war crime in the vicinity of Groß Tramken, Danzig; on or about the 27 March 1944.

Again, all three pleaded Not Guilty to the charges.

As the prosecution team was not fully prepared to proceed with the case it was deemed necessary to postpone it until later that year. The court was adjourned. Perhaps one of the reasons which contributed to the adjournment of the second trial was the case against Bruchhardt. McKenna leading the investigation had established the name of Venediger's driver as Peter Bontenbroich. In 1946 an all-out search began for him, but he wasn't caught until two years later. In July 1948, Sergeant Heron of the SIB arrested two Danzig drivers, Willi Reimer and Peter Bontenbroich.[52]

The second Sagan trial reconvened in October 1948 and proved far more efficient as there were only three men accused. Standing with Reinhold Bruchhardt were Erwin Wieczorek, Scharpwinkel's deputy in Breslau, and Richard Max Hänsel head of the Gestapo in Görlitz, on whom the Judge Advocate General considered there to be insufficient evidence in 1947. The court proceedings lasted twenty days from 11 October to 6 November 1948.

Kurt Lundehn

On the Sixth day of the Sagan trial, Kurt Lundehn was brought into the court to testify.

In 1944, he was working within the Danzig Gestapo for Department III and took part in the nationwide search. His particular role was to check the trains travelling between Danzig, Konitz and Dirschau. In court, he stated that he never made any arrests nor did he hear of any such arrests. This may not be that surprising given that almost 200 men worked in the Gestapo at that time, plus other units were seconded to the search such as the Kripo and the Volkssturm.

From his testimony, hearsay evidence was accepted in court which the prosecution needed to support the idea of a special murder squad which they wanted to prove had existed within the Danzig Gestapo. This was a useful argument for the prosecution. However, this arguably should not have been heard in court. This was debated at the time, but the witness was allowed to continue, and he put forward the names of those in this special squad—Asal, Hug, Voelz, all of whom were criminal assistants in Department III. The squad was led by Bruchhardt of Department II, who was the senior officer.

Lundehn stated that this information came from two NCOs who had been known to him, Wenzlaff and Weidmann.

---

[52] Allen Andrews, Exemplary Justice (London: Harrap 1976), p200.

Groß Trampken

At the trial, Lieutenant Colonel Barratt prosecuting, brought the attention of the court to Bruchhardt's changing testimony. When he had first arrived in England a statement was made, and this was perhaps mistranslated. At a later stage, a second statement was made by Bruchhardt, but investigators were unwilling to accept it. Almost certainly, the treatment that Bruchhardt received ensured that it was difficult for him to recall the events of some three years prior with any accuracy.

Bruchhardt was held in solitary and recalled in court how he was forced to work for 48 hours before he collapsed. Allegedly a 'Major Terry' had mistreated him by pulling out clumps of hair, repeatedly slapping and hitting him in the face in an attempt to break his nose. Under such conditions then anyone would find it difficult to remember details with any clarity.

In court, Barratt built the case for the prosecution by implying that Bruchhardt was constantly changing his statements in an attempt to show himself to be innocent. This, Barratt claimed, happened when Bruchhardt found out that the drivers Willi Reimer and Peter Bontenbroich were to be called as witnesses.

Bruchhardt – trial testimony

Reinhold Bruchhardt was born in the city of Danzig at a time when it was a German state, otherwise known as the Kingdom of Prussia. He learned the export trade and travelled to Brazil in 1932 but returned after a year to unemployment at a time of crisis in Germany. Unable to find gainful employment in Danzig, he opted to join the *Schutzstaffel* or 'SS'.

At that time, it was called the Free City of Danzig—also referred to as 'Area 26' by the German authorities, but it was not within Germany's borders at that time.

Bruchhardt's role with the SS was essentially unpaid guard duty, he worked simply in exchange for food and accommodation. After a few years, he joined the *Kriminalpolizei* to be able to have enough money to support his wife. Assigned to a department that supervised political parties, he was promoted to criminal assistant in April 1935. By now, all security officials were being pressured into joining the National Socialist Party (NSDAP), which he did in 1936.

With the invasion of Poland in September 1939, the free city was annexed into Germany. For Bruchhardt this resulted in promotion but also a change of status—he was now part of the *Geheime Staatspolizei*, the now-infamous Gestapo. Unhappy with this forced change to his police role, he twice applied for transfer to an active military unit and was twice refused.

Owing to a disagreement with a superior officer, he found himself being transferred out of his home city, first to Trior and then to Luxembourg. After two years he returned to Danzig and by this time the Gestapo chief was Günther Venediger. After a period in departments overseeing the press and party matters, Bruchhardt was transferred in 1943 to Department II Security. The main function of this department was to ensure the safety of visiting officials and other high-profile persons who would either visit the city because of its industrial importance, factories, shipyards, etc. or because they were transiting the area to reach Hitler's HQ at Rastenburg.

Under instruction from Berlin, Bruchhardt would form a squad of men to ensure the security of these individuals who would often be transiting the city at night. Trains travelling under the cover of darkness were more common than during daylight hours because of the risk from the air.

Spring 1944

On the fifteenth day of the trial, Bruchhardt's defending counsel, Dr Weber, changed his questioning to the subject of the events which occurred in the woods near Danzig. Asked about Spring 1944, Bruchhardt told the court that he was contacted at home by telephone in the early hours of the morning and requested to report to the Gestapo office by the duty official.

Bruchhardt rode his motorcycle the short distance to the office and, as requested, reported to Venediger, the head of the Gestapo. At this meeting, Venediger informed Bruchhardt that something unpleasant had just happened a short time earlier that day. Four British prisoners of war were being transported back to the camp from which they had escaped. Whilst being transported they had made another attempt to get away and were shot whilst trying to do so.

Venediger didn't doubt the report that he had received from the squad of men as he had earlier instructed the squad to use their weapons ruthlessly should any escape attempt be made by the four prisoners. Bruchhardt was then ordered to drive to the location, investigate the matter and take charge of the bodies. He was also instructed to take two men who had been involved with the nationwide search, so therefore two criminal police officials, Hug and Sasse, accompanied Bruchhardt to Groß Trampken.

While just a few kilometres short of the village, a driver by the name of Kurt Sommer flagged them down so they stopped. Sommer had been conscripted as a driver for the Gestapo at the beginning of the war. Bruchhardt said he was greeted with the following *'A pretty thing has happened here, these chaps wanted to run away, but not with us.'* [53] At the same time, Sommer indicated a wooded lane to the right-hand side of the road. The men walked together approximately fifty metres into the woods and they came upon four other Gestapo officials from Danzig.

Bruchhardt was unable to recall their names but believed they came from the department responsible for dealing with partisans. He explained not knowing their names by saying that there were many Gestapo officials from other places such as Bromberg, Graudenz, Thorn and Danzig. Many of these officials were working temporarily in Danzig or carrying out investigations in that area.

When asked what happened next, Bruchhardt confirmed that four officials were standing next to four bodies lying in the lane. Bruchhardt said when he looked at the four bodies he thought to himself how strange it seemed that they would be lying so close together. When he glanced at his subordinate officers, they appeared to be thinking the same thing.

A *Sturmscharführer*, whom Bruchhardt recognised also as a police officer, reported to him how the men had tried to run away. The officer went on to say the prisoners had previously been asked to relieve themselves but they took the opportunity to try and run away from their captors. Despite calls to halt, the prisoners didn't stop, so warning shots were fired, and these were followed by lethal shots.

Examining the corpses, Bruchhardt could see that most of the wounds were in the back, about 2-4 shots each. One of them had a bullet wound to the wrist and another had a flesh wound to the neck. The corpses were dressed in uniforms, khaki-battledress typical of that worn by British prisoners of war. Over this, the four men wore khaki greatcoats.

One of the officers that had accompanied Bruchhardt pointed out the footprints and drag marks which indicated that the men had been shot a short distance away and that they had been carried to where they now lay in the middle of the lane. Footprints of the escaping prisoners were distinctly visible in the snow. Where those tracks ended, the snow was covered in blood and more blood stains where the men had collapsed and died after they had been shot.

---

[53] United Nations War Crimes Commission. British Military Courts (S-1804-0160 -- S-1804-0173). UNWCC10.csv:763 https://www.legal-tools.org/

Bruchhardt had no reason to doubt that the earlier report received by Venediger in Danzig was indeed correct. With this, he dispatched one of the officials to Groß Trampken to report to the authorities there. A second official was ordered to the Gestapo office in Danzig to inform the duty officer to send a doctor to the scene. After that, the official was to arrange for a lorry to collect the bodies before reporting to Venediger about Bruchhardt's actions.

*

The first to arrive at the scene was Dr Parmann, at approximately 7.00 a.m., who quickly examined the bodies. The doctor checked for a pulse or a heartbeat and feeling neither confirmed that the men were dead. Once this was done, the doctor left the scene.

A lorry then arrived which was driven by one of the men from the motor pool. The driver was Willi Reimer who was instructed by Bruchhardt to reverse the lorry he was driving into the lane to make it easier to load the bodies into the vehicle. As this was happening, another Mercedes car arrived driven by Bontenbroich and carrying the Gestapo chief Günther Venediger.

When he was shown the bodies and the events of that morning were explained to him, he reportedly said the following *'We do not want to talk about this, and we do not want this to be made public. The best thing for you to do is to consider this a top-secret matter.'* [54] This was spoken to all of those officials present and ensured their agreement with a handclasp, binding them to silence.

Final instructions were given to the truck driver, Reimer, to inform Bruchhardt when the truck was back in the yard of the Gestapo HQ in Danzig. After this, Venediger left in a car, accompanied by Bruchhardt, driven by Bontenbroich.

*

On the sixteenth day of the Curiohaus trial, Bruchhardt was called again to take the stand. Although he was unsure of the actual details of the arrests, Bruchhardt stated that he knew the four prisoners were recaptured between Dirschau and Marienburg, or at least at a location close to Dirschau. This is consistent with the statement provided by Corporal Hicks who was at Stalag XX B.

---

[54] United Nations War Crimes Commission. British Military Courts (S-1804-0160 -- S-1804-0173). UNWCC10.csv:763 https://www.legal-tools.org/

Bontenbroich – the Gestapo driver's testimony

The driver Peter Bontenbroich was called as a witness. During the trial, he confirmed that he had been employed at the Danzig department of the Gestapo. There, he had been a Criminal Secretary, and he had been in charge of the motor pool. His duties also included being the regular driver for Günther Venediger since his arrival in 1943.

Although he was unable to recall the exact date, he was able to remember the morning he drove Venediger from Danzig to the forest near Groß Trampken. In his statement, he said they departed Danzig at 06.30 and after approximately 30 minutes they reached the place where Bruchhardt was waiting. He gave the time of their arrival as approximately 07.00.

From the testimony in court given by another witness, Dr Parmann, who confirmed that he received a telephone call at 06.00. During that telephone conversation, he was instructed to get himself ready to be taken somewhere for the purposes of examining some corpses. Shortly after the call he was picked up by a driver, and the journey to the scene took approximately thirty minutes.

In court, the defending counsel, Dr Weber, asked whether Bontenbroich knew of Dr Parmann and the witness claimed that he did not know him, nor would he have recognised him. Therefore, Bontenbroich was unable to say for sure whether or not the Parmann was present at the scene. However, the glaringly obvious fact is that Dr Parman was called and was either present or on his way to the scene when Bontenbroich arrived.

Weber asked Bontenbroich again if he was certain that he had heard shots, something which was not confirmed by any other witness. In reply, Bontenbroich said that he had come to the court to tell the truth and that he had heard the shots.

In his testimony, Bontenbroich said he drove Venediger to the scene. The vehicle was met at the side of the road by Bruchhardt, who was waiting at a crossroads next to where another lorry was parked. The crossroads was in an area of woodland, and both Venediger and Bruchhardt walked into the woods. Bontenbroich waited with the other driver, who he named as Piontke. After about five minutes Bontenbroich said that he felt bored. According to Bontenbroich, Piontke suggested that they should have a look at what was going on, and the pair walked a short distance along the path into the woods before hearing shots.

Map of the murder location near Groß Trampken drawn by Bontenbroich and used in court. [i]

This was the only point of difference between the case for the prosecution and that of the defence. If the doctor had been called, then the men were already dead. Piontke was not called as a witness to confirm Bontenbroich's testimony in court.

Willi Reimer and Peter Bontenbroich proved to be vital witnesses in the prosecution's case for the Danzig murders and both gave evidence which led to Bruchhardt's conviction.

Reimer's testimony was not disputed in court; he arrived in a lorry to collect the corpses for transport back to Gestapo headquarters. In his statement, both Venediger and Bruchhardt were standing by the side of the road so Reimer must have arrived after Bontenbroich. Several witnesses confirmed Venediger and Bruchhardt had been present at the scene, but it was only Bontenbroich who claimed to have heard shots. This is the only testimony which puts Venediger and Bruchhardt at the scene when the murders were committed. This would also mean that the doctor was called before the killings and that a report was not made to Venediger in Danzig earlier that morning.

But what if Bontenbroich had simply intended to implicate his superior officer?

*

One of the five other suspects who had been identified by Bontenbroich in his testimony as being present at the scene of the murders was Hans Asal who was picked up by the SIB and interviewed. Asal was a Gestapo official in Danzig and subordinate to Bruchhardt.

He gave his statement to the investigators.

'I can't remember when the case with the English aviators took place. According to my memory, it must have been in the spring of 1943 (sic). I still remember that a large-scale manhunt was triggered back then (wanted level alpha). I also remember that the photographs of the escaped officers were printed in the supplement to the German criminal police newspaper. However, there were not 100 officers, but only around 50.

I don't know anything about the further events in this matter. It could very well be that I learned from a conversation that four of the escaped officers had been picked up in the Danzig area. I don't know anything else. In particular, I did not know at the time that the four officers had been shot.

If it is alleged to me that (the driver) Reimer stated that, according to his memory, which is not reliable, I was also in the forest in which the four officers were shot, then that is incorrect. I am told that I could also make use of my right to refuse to testify in accordance with Section 55, but I have no reason to do so; in fact, I can declare with a clear conscience that I had nothing to do with the shooting of the four officers. I also don't know how the matter was handled internally at the Gestapo and what role the accused Dr Venediger played there.

Besides, I am not surprised that it is Reimer who suspected me of this.

Because of this matter, I was arrested by the British on 1 July 1948 and kept in custody until 6 December 1948. At that time, it was pointed out to me that Bontenbroich had stated that I was probably involved in the shooting of the airmen. It strikes me that the accusation made by Bontenbroich at the time corresponds almost word for word to the information that Reimer gave during his interrogation by the Cloppenburg criminal police on 8 August 1949. In any case, the English were convinced that I had nothing to do with this matter, which is why I was released after half a year's custody in Hamburg.

I can't say where the Hug, Roehrer, Sasse and Fels mentioned by Reimer are. I know them all because they also worked for the border police. I last saw them in the days of the collapse.' Hans ASAL[55]

*

Alexander Scotland was determined to find someone responsible for the murders near Danzig and he was convinced that Bruchhardt was his man. During the trial, as well as confirming the key details of the investigation, Scotland presented his testimony for the prosecution against the accused. During the course of the investigation led by Scotland, a statement was given by Bruchhardt whilst he was under duress. When he later tried to provide a second statement, this was allegedly rejected by Scotland, who simply refused to accept it.

During the trial various aspects of these separate statements were discussed and issues of the translation of certain passages within them. Some of the translations appeared to be less favourable in portraying Bruchhardt's testimony. In court Bruchhardt was unable to remember writing paragraphs in one of the statements, suggesting that this was due to the ill-treatment he received before he wrote his statement.

---

[55] Archives of the Pilecki Institute. Warsaw. IP/Arch/7/35.8.10.2/756. Access date 23.11.2023. Creator's ref no: B162/27885. Bundesarchiv. Zentrale Stelle der Landesjustizverwaltungen zur Aufklärung nationalsozialistischer Verbrechen.

Furthermore, in court, a witness provided the name of Kurt Achterberg as Günther Venediger's deputy and it was Achterberg who had been very keen to divert any attention from himself by giving the investigators Bruchhardt's name. This might also have been done as an act of revenge against the man who was having an affair with Achterburg's wife at the time.

Scotland would also have been aware that should a conviction not be obtained, then it would be almost certainly impossible for the SIB to continue the investigation and to find other suspects. The political climate in the United Kingdom and Germany was changing quickly, and the British government's appetite for prosecuting war criminals was fading fast.

*

At the end of the trial proceedings, the prosecution summed up its case. The issue was whether the defendant had arrived at the scene before or after the shooting had taken place—Bruchhardt confirmed that he was at the scene on Venediger's orders, but only after the men had been killed. It was Bontenbroich who claimed that Venediger and Bruchhardt walked into the woods together before he heard shots— also admitting that he did not witness what took place. From the timeline, confirmed by Dr Parmann, then there was a strong probability that the men were already dead when Bontenbroich arrived at the scene of the murders in the woods.

It was solely on the driver's testimony that the accusation as to whether Bruchhardt was in charge of a special murder squad and guilty of the crimes was based. Bruchhardt claimed that the murders were carried out by a special detachment led by an official from Bromberg, he was so convinced of this that he was willing to search for those responsible if he was allowed to do so. There was no material evidence presented in court, no forensics, and no reliable witnesses to state categorically that it was Bruchhardt acting as the senior officer who ordered the executions.

And yet, Bruchhardt was found guilty as charged.

In the final arguments made by Dr Weber, the defence counsel for Bruchhardt, he said that it was his belief that the court should not make use of its power to give the death sentence. He was not an adherent of capital punishment and he referred to recent discussions in the Houses of Parliament. Additionally, the British Court was administering justice in Hamburg which had a long tradition of not carrying out death sentences. He gave a further reason why capital punishment should not apply in this case—there was not yet peace between Great Britain and Germany referring to a general feeling within the German population 'that we have to get along with

England'. He added that the punishment should not be in revenge, and a wider situation should be considered.

Bruchhardt was allowed to speak, and he restated his innocence concerning the deaths of these officers. He had also not been in any position to call any character witnesses or those who could confirm his version of events.

Bruchhardt was sentenced to be hanged.

*

As the trial of Reinhold Bruchhardt, Richard Hänsel, and Erwin Wieczorek had been delayed for fifteen months whilst the prosecution built its case then this may have kept them alive. Hänsel was found not guilty of the charges he faced. Although Wieczorek was sentenced to death on 6 November 1948, this conviction was quashed on review.

Bruchhardt's death sentence was commuted to life imprisonment, and after serving less than eight years he was released under a general amnesty. In 1938, the British Government debated the issue of capital punishment. This was revived in 1948 at the time of the war trials in Hamburg.

The second trial concluded at a time when capital punishment was losing support and when relations between the countries of Germany and Great Britain were changing from victor and vanquished to becoming something more cooperative in the face of increasing tensions between East and West at the beginning of the Cold War.

Thirteen officials who had been condemned for their involvement in the Sagan murders died on the hangman's rope. Some of them were not brutal killers but men forced to carry out the orders which they had been given. Reinhold Bruchhardt, of the Danzig Gestapo, was certainly not an innocent man but his guilt in these murders was not shown to be beyond any reasonable doubt.

Bruchardt's stubborn silence over nearly two years had saved his life. His statement that the murders had been committed by a Ukrainian execution squad was finally refuted when Reimer and Bontenbroich, driver-mechanics to Venediger and Bruchardt, swore to having driven them to Groß Trampken, a wood near Danzig, where the four officers were shot. [56]

That Bruchhardt had been the leader of a special squad was hearsay. His direct superior also testified at the trial and stated that he was unaware of any execution squad.

---

[56] Allen Andrews, Exemplary Justice (London: Harrap 1976), p257.

The United Kingdom abandoned the death penalty.

In 1938 the issue of the abolition of capital punishment was brought before parliament. A clause within the Criminal Justice Bill called for an experimental five-year suspension of the death penalty. When war broke out in 1939 the bill was postponed, before being revived after the war in 1948. Somewhat surprisingly, this was adopted by a majority in the House of Commons. In the House of Lords, the abolition clause was defeated but the remainder of the bill was passed as the Criminal Justice Act 1948.

By 1957, a number of controversial cases highlighted the issue of capital punishment again. Several individuals were executed too quickly as later trials and prosecutions cast huge doubts on those convictions. Campaigners for abolition were partially rewarded with the Homicide Act 1957. The Act brought in a distinction between capital and non-capital murder.

Questions were asked in Parliament.

The work of the London Cage was under a cloud of suspicion. Had the interrogators mistreated those whom they suspected of being guilty? Various reports reached the press and at the trial in Hamburg, the accused Bruchhardt was reluctant to talk of the treatment which he had received at the Cage.

Questions were raised in the British Parliament by Mr Paget, a Member of the House, regarding the goings on at the secret facility in the heart of London.

Mr. Paget

The MP asked the Secretary of State for War whether he has considered the declarations by Reinhold Bruchhardt and others concerning cruel methods adopted by the London District Cage during 1946 to secure statements and confessions; and whether, in view of these statements, he will order a full and public inquiry into the administration of that Cage.

Mr. M. Stewart

The only declarations by Bruchhardt alleging cruelties at London District Cage of which I am aware are allegations made at his trial, on which the counsel for the defence cross-examined one of the witnesses, and the statement dated 13th September 1948, sent by my honourable and learned Friend. This statement was prepared between 28th

August 1948, when Bruchhardt was arraigned, and 11th October, when his trial started; it appears to be a document prepared for the purpose of briefing the German counsel who was to defend him; it supplied the material for the few questions about alleged cruelties at London District Cage which the counsel for the defence put to one of the witnesses at the trial; the defence did not press the matter.

Similar allegations were made by some of the accused who were tried in the first Stalag Luft 3 trial during the summer of 1947. The allegations made at this trial were investigated with the greatest care by the court which heard the evidence of some Germans who had nothing to do with the case but who alleged that they had been ill-treated at London District Cage. The trial (in which there were 18 accused) took 50 working days. All the accused were convicted, and it follows in the circumstances of the case that the court rejected the contention that the statements made by the accused at the London District Cage were induced by ill-treatment.

In all the circumstances my right honourable Friend does not propose to institute any further inquiry into the allegations referred to in the Question.

Günther Venediger went to ground

The identity card used by Venediger.[ii]

Günther Venediger had been responsible for issuing the orders and was guilty of orchestrating the killings of Walenn and the other three officers. However, he was still beyond the reach of British justice.

From 15 August 1941, Venediger headed the Danzig State Police Headquarters. At the time of the Sagan murders, he was the senior official and thereby responsible for anything that transpired under his jurisdiction. It is clear from the various testimonies that he certainly orchestrated the killings of Walenn and his three fellow escapers.

From Bontenbroich's testimony during the trials, we know that he claimed to have witnessed Venediger and Bruchhardt walk into the woods before hearing shots fired. No other witness confirmed this, but whether Venediger was present when the killings took place or not, he issued the orders for others to carry out. Perhaps intentionally, he distanced himself from the crime by using others, but he was culpable for the murders. Venediger was a guilty man and he was still unaccounted for.

*

In November 1943, Venediger gained promotion to SS-*Obersturmbannführer* and the position of senior government councillor. From 1944 he was also commander of the security police and the SD in Danzig. Under his authority, Venediger was responsible for over two hundred admissions to the Stutthof concentration camp near Danzig. Documents also show that he was involved in murders such as the shooting of hostages. In one such case, at his instigation, three Poles were hanged for allegedly having sexual intercourse with a German woman.[57]

In March 1945, with the Russians advancing from the east, Venediger decided it was time to leave Danzig and he hid on a farm near the city for a week. Accepting that defeat was imminent, he sought to save his skin by abandoning his post. Others had been summarily executed for desertion in the face of the enemy.

Karl Otto Moritz Feodor Georg von Salisch was a German police officer and SS-*Standartenführer*. From 1942 to 1945, Salisch served as Chief of Police of Bromberg, also in departments of the Reich Security Main Office. After Salisch had withdrawn from his area of command in January 1945 in the face of advancing Soviet troops, he was arrested and summarily sentenced for desertion and 'cowardice'.

On 31 January 1945 in the courtyard of the Danzig Gestapo, Salisch was executed by firing squad, which was ordered by Venediger and the squad was led by Bruchhardt. Of course, they were both carrying out orders from a higher authority, that of Heinrich Himmler.

Venediger headed west and reached Swinemünde and from there to Schwerin, where he briefly stayed at the alternate location of the Imperial Governor of Danzig-West Prussia. He then reached the Gestapo's alternative headquarters in Flensburg, where he met *Reichsführer* SS Heinrich Himmler who appointed Venediger as SS-*Standartenführer*. With the now obvious imminent total collapse of the Third Reich, at the beginning of May 1945, he acquired false papers adopting the identity of 'Paul Schaller' and left Flensburg.

After the German capitulation, he hid himself within the English occupation zone under another false identity, that of 'August Nieder.' Using this name, he worked as a farmhand on an estate near Goslar in Lower Saxony until July 1952.

In October 1952 he was recognised in Stuttgart. Detained by the police, he was released after interrogation and worked as a commercial clerk in Düsseldorf.

---

[57] Dieter Schenk, Danzig 1930–1945 The end of a free city (Berlin: Christoph Links, 2013), p141-143.

Erich Graes – later testimony

On 4 August 1949, as part of the proceedings against Venediger, Erich Graes gave a further statement to the police in Bottrop. At the time, it was in the British Sector of Germany, located in west-central Germany, in the Ruhr industrial area.

According to Graes' statement, because of the shooting of four English military officers in Danzig, he was arrested by the English in 1945. He was interned by the military and later taken to England. There he was questioned several times about this matter in London.

Four of the escaped officers were recaptured by a Wehrmacht patrol on a passenger train near Konitz. The military patrol then delivered the four Englishmen to a prisoner of war camp in Marienburg—Stalag XX B. There the men were issued with new ID cards with their correct names. Although Graes was unsure of the exact details of the arrests or the length of stay in Marienburg, he was sure that it couldn't have been more than 2-3 days.

As the matter progressed, instructions were received from the Reich Criminal Police Office. As Graes was the deputy head of the criminal police in Danzig, he issued orders after the receipt of a direct and secret message from his superiors in Berlin.

According to instructions, the four officers were taken from the Stalag by the Criminal Commissioner Gleisberg and some other officials. It was considered likely that they might attempt to escape again and therefore care was to be used in their transport. Graes arranged for the British officers to be held in a better room following the Geneva Convention on the treatment of prisoners of war. They were put into escape-proof cells whilst officials waited for further orders. Graes left the office and was taken to his apartment around 11 p.m. and at that time he was informed that the four airmen were on their way from Marienburg (Stalag XX B/Willenberg).

Graes recalled that the officers were accommodated in the police prison in Danzig for one night and then transferred to another camp. As they had been brought in late in the evening Graes had no contact with them. Arriving at the office the following morning, he asked the head of the police prison whether everything was in order but was informed that the four English officers had been picked up by members of the Gestapo during the night.

*

In this statement, Graes confirmed that he was born on May 5, 1901, in Cologne, and at that time he lived in Bottrop, Scharnholzstr 47, Germany.

Once familiarised with the subject matter of the police witness interrogation and once warned to be careful, he explained the following:

'Before my transfer in 1943, I was in the Criminal Police active in Magdeburg. With my promotion to Criminal Director, I was transferred to Danzig and began my service there as deputy director on April 25, 1943. The head was the senior government councillor, Friedrich Hermann. Hermann was there around August 1944, when the Stapo leader Dr Venediger was appointed commander of the security police and was transferred to Stuttgart. From that day on I became head of Department V (criminal police) in Danzig.

Authorities:

1) Higher SS and Pol. Leader (Group Leader Katzmann)
2) Inspector of the Security Police and SD (Brigade Leader Willich)
3) SD control section (Dr Steinbacher *Ober-Sturmbannführer*)
4) State Pol. Control Centre (Senior Government Councillor Dr Venediger)
5) Criminal Pol. Control Centre (Senior Government Councillor Hermann)

In August 1944, the inspector was appointed commander and at the same time received the additional rank of major general of the police. The Stapo leader Dr Venediger was appointed commander of the security police, the previous state police control centre became Department IV, and the previous Criminal police control centre became Department V of the commander of the security police.

During my time in Danzig, I never tolerated any mistreatment of detainees, and I also told my department heads this. I have never heard of any infringement by one of my officials in this area. I would like to note that the detainees from the criminal police were housed exclusively in the Police Prison, which was in the Police Presidium.

Because of the shooting of four English military officers in Danzig, I was arrested by the English Military government interned and brought to England in 1945. I was questioned on this matter several times in London. Very briefly what happened:

Around 100 English people escaped from the Sagan camp. Pilot officers broke out, four of whom were caught by a purely military patrol on a passenger train near Konitz. They were transferred to the Marienburg Stalag. The Criminal police found out about this fact through a message from Berlin, in which they were asked to pick up these four officers from the camp.

They were to be accommodated in the police prison in Danzig for one night and then transferred to another camp. According to instructions, the four officers were taken by the Criminal Commissioner Gleisberg and some officials were picked up after the police prison had previously been instructed to prepare a dignified room for the accommodation within the framework of the Geneva Convention. The officers were brought in late in the evening and when we asked the police prison the next morning whether everything was in order, we were told that these four officers had been picked up by members of the Stapo during the night. Hermann immediately asked the Stapo, who cited a secret command matter. A few days later, Hermann received a message from Berlin, in which he was asked to have the four urns of the four officers shot while trying to escape brought to Breslau.

I had a detailed discussion with Hermann at the time about this matter, which was a travesty of the Geneva Convention, and we were in complete agreement about condemning such a solution. But we avoided talking to the Stapo about it.'

The Trials of Günther Venediger

In October 1952, Venediger was arrested after he was recognised in Stuttgart. Although he was detained by the local police, he was released after questioning.

Proceedings for his complicity in the murders were opened against him on five separate occasions and closed each time. These prosecutions were no longer under the jurisdiction of a British military court but were now carried out under the German civilian legal system. It is worth noting that many judges and lawyers who held positions during the time of the Nazis retained their status and transitioned into the post-war legal system.

The overriding issue of the prosecutions was simply whether the accused was aware of the illegality of the orders issued by the Reich Security Main Office (RSHA). It goes without saying, that he must have known at the time the prisoners had been executed without any court trial. However, no main proceedings were opened against Venediger because his defence maintained that at the time of the murders, he was unable to recognise the illegality of these executions ordered by the RSHA.

In a later case, in December 1953, Venediger was charged with accessory to quadruple murder before the Heilbronn jury court for the shooting of the British officers near Danzig. On direct instructions from the RSHA, the four men were picked up by officers under Venediger's command and shot near Groß Trampken. Venediger claimed that he was only following orders and was allegedly unable to prove at that time the illegality of those orders.

The 1953 trial accusations [iii]

Against Dr Venediger is accused of being in Danzig and the surrounding area in 1941 and 1945.

1. having killed people insidiously and cruelly or having caused them to be killed,
2. as a civil servant, having intentionally committed or ordered bodily harm in the exercise of his office,
3. as an official, intentionally making or ordering arrests and arrests without having the right to do so,
4. as an official in investigations, having used or ordered coercive measures in order to extort confessions and statements,
5. as an official superior, having intentionally induced his subordinates to commit criminal acts in office,
6. as head of the Gestapo in Danzig, mistreatment of prisoners for the purpose of blackmailing statements from the Gestapo office

The shooting of four British airmen

In the evening or early night hours of that day—the exact date is not certain, a telex from the RSHA, Amt IV (Secret State Police) arrived at the state police control centre in Danzig with the Signature of the department head SS-Gruppenführer Müller. It was a secret message addressed to Dr Günther Venediger, Head of the Department. Since this was a secret Reich matter, the witness Hermann Juhl, who operated the teleprinter, had to be called back into the office to deal with the message.

Juhl was unable to recall the exact wording of the message, but the essential content of the message was 'on the orders of the Führer, the four refugees listed by name who are in the custody of the Danzig Criminal Investigation Department were to be shot after their identity had been verified. This was to be done on namely 'on the run', i.e. outwardly under the pretext that they were shot trying to escape. After the execution of the command, a completion report was to be sent to Berlin. It was further stipulated that the telex, which had no number and was not allowed to be recorded in the log book, should be destroyed by the department leader. Juhl took the secret telex and immediately passed it on to the Gestapo chief, Günther Venediger.

As Venediger read the telex he claimed his first thought was, 'For God's sake, what will happen to our captives?' Presumably thinking of those men held by the Allies. He knew that this action was forbidden under the Geneva Convention, and should the

Allies become convinced that officers had been murdered then similar reprisals might be considered by the British Government.

According to the Geneva Convention, it was forbidden to shoot prisoners of war. However, if a prisoner was trying to escape then lethal force could be used. Despite measures of secrecy, it could become known that prisoners were murdered and corresponding measures by the Allies against German prisoners of war in their custody could follow. At this stage of the war, particularly after the collapse of German forces in North Africa, many German POWs were in English hands.

Although Venediger was aware that the killing he had been ordered to do was illegal it had come from the highest authority, Adolf Hitler, and he felt that it could not be refused without consequences. He decided to take responsibility for giving the orders to carry out these executions.

Venediger had the four English officers brought from the criminal police jail and taken to his office building, the Gestapo HQ. When they arrived, he glanced once into the room where they were held but claimed that he did not speak to them. He then issued orders to one of his officers to carry out the shooting with some people from the anti partisan squad as ordered. He also decided upon the location, namely the forest near Groß Trampken, about twenty kilometres south of Danzig, and added instructions about how the killings were to be carried out. He stayed in the office building overnight and in the early morning hours after dusk, Venediger was informed by telephone that the orders had been carried out.

It was not possible to determine who directed the shooting at the scene. The witness Bruchhardt, who was sentenced to death as the leader of a special squad by an English military court in 1948 and who was released after his pardon, always disputed the accuracy of the military court's findings. In addition to him, there was also a 'criminal secretary JAPS' who allegedly led the anti-partisan squad at the time.

There is no doubt that the witness Bruchhardt was at the crime scene at least afterwards and saw the dead men. The bullets had hit the officers and the bodies had bullet holes in their backs. They lay on the right and left of a forest track in the Groß Trampken woods not far from a country road, a distance of about twenty metres into the woods. Traces of blood and drag marks could be seen in the snow, leading from where they had collapsed to the spot where the bodies were dragged.

Venediger also admitted to visiting the shooting site early in the morning. A witness at the trial in Hamburg, Bontenbroich, who was Venediger's regular driver confirmed that they had driven to the murder site. On the return journey, in addition to Venediger, the witness Bruchhardt also rode in the vehicle. Bruchhardt got off at a bridge in Danzig and walked to the office, while Bontenbroich took Venediger to his apartment to have breakfast.

The SS and police doctor from Danzig, a Dr Parmann, confirmed the deaths of the four officers in the forest, and the responsible mayor's office was ordered to issue a certificate stating that the four had been shot while trying to escape. The bodies were transported in a truck to the state police headquarters building. There, house prisoners placed the bodies in four coffins.

'It may have been in March 1944 when around one hundred English airmen escaped from the Sagan prison camp. Such prison escapes had reached a frightening extent at the time. It was also known that the prisoners who had escaped got into contact with some underground movements, so for this reason, state security was being investigated.

A large-scale manhunt was then launched because of the English people who had escaped. We assumed it was fairly certain that some of those who had escaped would try to make their way to Danzig; this was simply because there were ship connections between the port of Danzig and Sweden. The refugees could hope to reach England via Sweden. The fact is that the four pilots were caught in the Danzig area, and they were handed over to the criminal police.

Today I no longer know whether I learned about this on-duty or off-duty. The criminal police then received instructions from Berlin from the Reich Criminal Police Office that the four pilots were to be handed over to the Gestapo. In the evening hours, a designated flash telex from the Reich Main Security Office arrived.

Probably on the same day, I received a secret Reich document with the signature of Müller, Head of Office IV, which stated that 'the four arrested airmen were to be shot on the order of the Führer himself.' I therefore became involved in the matter and gave the commands to a certain number of men to shoot the recaptured airmen.

I admit that this order from Hitler did not seem harmless to me. This was at least because of the possible consequences that this could have for German prisoners on the other side. It was in this spirit that I spoke out against Willich back then. I can no longer say today whether I gave any further thought to how such an order could be reconciled with the principles of international law. If I had made such considerations, they would probably have taken a back seat to the idea that the war had now taken on forms that in many cases could no longer be reconciled with any legal norms.

I was always particularly shocked when I saw or heard about the devastating effects of the Allied air raids on the German civilian population. I have also already indicated above the danger that escaped prisoners of war tried to collude with foreign underground movements on a large scale. Of course, these were things that I was unable to understand in their entirety. But if I received such an order from the highest leadership of the Reich, then I had to assume without further ado that it was based on compelling considerations in the interests of national defence or state security.

I have to be very resolute against the suggestion that I acted 'out of hatred'. Of course, I never felt such an emotion towards any of the airmen captured here, just as soldiers in general don't usually feel any real hatred towards their opponents. Rather, I was honestly convinced that there were state-political necessities for Hitler's order, which I neither had nor could examine in detail. In this respect, I was absolutely convinced of the legality of the order.

The thought that I could practically not evade the implementation of the decision that had come from an order of the highest level was, if at all, of only minor importance to me.

In fact, there would have been no such possibility of disobedience. If, for example, I had wanted to make my office unavailable, I would have been arrested on the spot and brought before the SS and police court, which would undoubtedly have immediately brought the death penalty.

I stopped short of describing what happened outside of the fact that I had received the telex with the execution order in the evening hours. I went with this order to Willich, who was still in his office. The purpose of my interview was to inform Willich about this matter, which was, after all, of particular importance. In this dissatisfaction, I have expressed the concerns I have already stated above. Willich shared my concerns but said that I would not allow the order to be carried out. As far as I can still remember, I then gave the commission to Criminal Secretary Bruchhardt to carry out the order. I can no longer say exactly whether this was Bruchhardt. When Bruchhardt states that the order was carried out by the Criminal Secretary JAPS, I do not want to doubt the correctness of this statement. I certainly did not give the officer in question any individual instructions regarding how to carry out the shooting. I just remember that we agreed that the shooting should take place outside of Danzig.

I was not present at the shooting itself. It wasn't until the next morning, as I remember from Bruchhardt, that I was told that the four Englishmen had been shot. I also don't know anything about the method of execution. In any case, one thing is clear to me: the shooting was not associated with any unnecessary torture. The enforcement report was then immediately sent to Berlin by telex. Immediately afterwards, instructions came from Berlin to take the bodies to the crematorium in Danzig, to be burned and the urns to be handed over to the criminal police. This happened too. As I later heard, the urns were said to have been taken to the prison camp in Sagan and buried there.

Regarding the statement of Mr. Graes, I don't have anything else to say. If the witness states that the urns should have been brought to Breslau, then I could have been wrong.

Regarding the statement by Reimer, I have already stated in my police interrogation that I was not present at the execution myself. Apart from that, Reimer's saying that he had the order to collect the bodies from the forest and bring them back to Danzig which is correct. I remember the names Hug, Rohrer, Sasse, Fels and Asal mentioned by Reimer. But I can't say whether these officials took part in the shooting.

If I myself spoke of a decree from Himmler in my police interrogation on page 106, that was wrong. As I stated the day before yesterday, the decree was signed by Müller. However, the original order was given by Hitler himself.

As far as I know, this was also made clear in the Nuremberg Process, in which the so-called Sagan case took up a lot of space.' [58]

The trial verdict

Dr Günther Venediger Venediger was acquitted on September 3, 1954. The prosecution had been unable to prove that he wasn't simply following orders from a higher authority. This prompted the head of the RAF investigation, Wilfred Bowes, to launch a cascade of indignant letters, and this may have had an influence on the public prosecutor's office.

The prosecution appealed against the decision because, in their opinion, Venediger should have recognised the illegality of the order he had received, and the alleged emergency of the order was also questionable. The public prosecutor's office had demanded a five-year prison sentence. For these reasons, the Federal Court of Justice referred the case back to the court in Heilbronn, where the case was heard again and

---

[58] Archives of the Pilecki Institute. Warsaw. IP/Arch/7/35.8.10.2/755. Access date 23.11.2023. Creator's ref no: B162/27884. Bundesarchiv. Zentrale Stelle der Landesjustizverwaltungen zur Aufklärung nationalsozialistischer Verbrechen.

Venediger was again acquitted in November 1955. After a further appeal, the case was reopened and brought before the Stuttgart regional court.

During his last trial, Venediger confirmed that he had the four English officers brought from the criminal police building and to his office building. Although he glanced once into the room where they were held, he claimed that he did not speak to them. Venediger admitted that he ordered one of his officers to carry out the shooting with officials from the anti-resistance squad and that the men were to be shot trying 'to escape'. He also named the location, namely the forest near Groß Trampken, about twenty kilometres south of Danzig. Venediger chose to remain in his office building overnight and in the early morning hours after dusk he was informed by telephone that the order had been carried out. Perhaps it was at that point, he contacted Bruchhardt and asked him to investigate.

On March 30, 1957, after five years of investigation and interrogation of his former collaborators from the Gestapo office in Danzig, the Stuttgart Regional Court sentenced Venediger to two years in prison for aiding and abetting manslaughter. The lenient punishment was judicially ascribed to the fact that he had not recognised the illegality of the superior orders he claimed to have been obeying. It was also claimed that he did not follow the order reluctantly.[59]

This verdict was only reached after pressure had been exerted on the German government. No other charges were brought against him, and no further investigations were conducted.

---

[59] Andreas Eichmüller, No general amnesty - The prosecution of Nazi crimes in the early Federal Republic (Munich, 2012), p337.

Not so Exemplary Justice

On 17th November 1948 Wing Commander Bowes wrote to the Provost Marshal:

It has been announced by the Cabinet that no further trials of war criminals will take place. In the particular case of the Stalag Luft 3 crime it would be a grave miscarriage of justice to allow these men to go free merely because, so far, they have been able to escape arrest whilst men less guilty have been executed. It is suggested that authority be sought to enable Judge Advocate General War Crimes to prosecute any of these prisoners in the event of their being arrested at some future date. [60]

Testimonies from German personnel during the post-war investigations and trials were often contradictory. Not entirely surprising, as those making the statements were only too aware that implicating themselves was likely to lead to conviction and possible execution.

The discovery of the complex chain of events from Hitler's order to execute all recaptured prisoners to those passing on these instructions and those responsible for carrying them out was an immense task that the investigation team had to achieve in a condensed timeframe. Given the state of post-war Europe at the time it is highly laudable that any of the suspects were found and prosecuted before the courts. The RAF Special Investigation Branch deserve every credit for their determination and persistence in bringing those guilty men to justice.

The then Foreign Secretary Anthony Eden, who later became Prime Minister, promised that those responsible would face 'Exemplary Justice'. As suspects became identified and cases against them were built, not all were brought to trial. Many of these former secret police officials used false identities and escaped detection. Others were killed during the closing stages of the war or committed suicide before or during arrest. It is suspected that some, like Wilhelm Scharpwinkel the Breslau Gestapo Chief, may have later worked for the Soviet intelligence agencies, although he did not leave for Russia willingly.

Justice served?

Reinhold Bruchhardt was sentenced to death on 6 November 1948, but this was commuted to life imprisonment, and he was released in 1956. After release from prison, Bruchhardt lived in Herford, Germany, where he eventually died in January 1979, nearly thirty-five years after the murders in the woods near Groß Trampken.

---

[60] Allen Andrews, Exemplary Justice (London: Harrap 1976), p258.

Dr Günther Venediger was head of the Danzig Gestapo. He was an SS Standartenführer, Oberreigerungsrat and Commander of the Sischerheitspolizei. He spent just two years in prison. After that he was allowed to live out his life, he divorced in 1967, and later died in April 1983 in Düsseldorf.

Romas Marcinkus had been a talented footballer, Gordon Brettell had a promising career as a motor racing driver, Henri Picard had chosen a military career, and Gilbert Walenn was a banker with a love of flying. All of these young men had their lives interrupted by the war and all four were murdered in cold blood following the escape from Stalag Luft 3. They had not committed any crime and their murders contravened the rules of war. And yet, none of those suspected or accused of being involved in the conspiracy to commit their murders received the death sentence. All escaped the hangman.

Hans Asal was a supposed member of the Danzig murder squad of Dr Venediger, he was located in the French zone, subsequently handed over, and released after interrogation. Weyland of Reichenberg was located inside the Russian zone and stayed there securely. Weissman of Reichenberg was also located in the French zone but was not transferred.

In March 1950 Wing Commander Bowes brought the attention of the Provost Marshal to the fact that Oskar Schafer, former Chief of the Gestapo at Munich, had been acquitted by a German court on charges of the killing of East European slave labourers, but had not been charged with the murders of Lieutenants Gouws and Stevens of the South African Air Force. The SIB traced the man who had earlier been freed to the British zone, and Bowes applied fresh pressure for further charges, which were not brought.

The matter was not abandoned by the German Prosecutor, but after eighteen years, on 11th December 1968, the Munich Court finally threw out the case. Despite the clear evidence at the original trial that Schafer had not only ordered and planned the murders of Lieutenants Gouws and Stevens but had ordered the erasure of the records. The men who gave this evidence originally had been hanged many years before.

For some of those fifty airmen who were murdered after The Great Escape, it seems that they did not receive justice—whether exemplary or otherwise.

The British Prosecution of Crimes in Hamburg

For other crimes that were committed, in the first 4 years after the war British military courts in Hamburg sentenced 366 people to death, and other defendants were given prison terms for their roles in committing Nazi crimes. These convictions, compared to the number of people who were prosecuted in East and West Germany in the decades following, show us that the Allied effort to punish criminals was highly determined given the difficult circumstances in post-war Europe.

The German Federal Republic formed after the war firmly refused to pass a special criminal law modelled after the Allies to punish Nazi crimes, and the Allies' innovations were not adopted into West German criminal legislation. This led to inconsistencies in terms of the prosecution of crimes in West Germany for decades after the war. Countless proceedings were stayed, and many courts issued extremely lenient sentences.

One thing is certain, all of those who were involved in those crimes are now dead.

Those implicated from Danzig [61]

Gestapo Chief Günther Venediger was sentenced in 1957 to two years in prison for aiding and abetting manslaughter.

Criminal Secretary Reinhold Bruchhardt was sentenced to life imprisonment in November 1948, after a British experimental suspension of the death penalty was introduced; in the end, he only served just under 8 years in prison.

Walter Sasse – Escaped from custody, untraced.

Julius Hug – Untraced.

Walter Voelz – Untraced.

Max Kilpe – Charges were dropped in August 1948 after the British government policy decision not to prosecute any further Nazi war criminals.

Herbert Wenzler – Charges were dropped in August 1948 after the British government policy decision not to prosecute any further Nazi war criminals.

Harold Witt – Charges were dropped in August 1948 after the British government policy decision not to prosecute any further Nazi war criminals.

*

McKenna knew a precept was at stake; 'exemplary justice,' to quote Anthony Eden's pledge, had been achieved. Not by lynchings and summary executions, but by the slow and relentless process of the law. Twenty-one Gestapo were executed, eleven committed suicide, six were killed by air raids in the last days of the war; seventeen received long sentences of imprisonment, a handful were acquitted; Scharpwinkel remained in Soviet hands and is alleged to have died in 1947. Friedrich Schmidt, the Kiel Gestapo chief, escaped prosecution until 1968 when he was arraigned before a German court and sentenced to two years imprisonment. His plea: he was only obeying orders.

The Longest Tunnel. Alan Burgess.

---

[61] Stephen R. Davies, A Global History of the RAF Police vol 5 (Kindle: 2012), p. 170.

Summary of Key Points

Although this is widely believed, Walenn, Marcinkus, Picard and Brettell were not recaptured in the region of Schneidemühl. Both Bruchhardt and Graes were sure that the four escaped airmen were picked up somewhere in the vicinity of Konitz, or between Konitz and Dirschau. This was confirmed in the statement by Erich Graes– *'the four officers were recaptured in the Danzig region and discovered on a train somewhere near Konitz.'*

Konitz is now known as Chojnice and lies just 120 kilometres from Malbork (formerly Marienburg). To put this into perspective, the distance between Schneidemühl and Marienburg was approximately two hundred and fifty kilometres by rail and therefore Konitz was considerably closer to the Stalag in Marienburg.

At the Stalag, Corporal Hicks encountered the men. If he recalled this correctly, then the escapers were even closer as Hicks said the men had been *'caught in the neighbourhood of Dirschau'*—a distance of just twenty kilometres from the camp.

Hicks described the men—*'the spokesman had a bushy, black moustache and an English accent'* a fair description of Walenn. Hicks also remembered that the spokesman mentioned one of his fellow officers was Belgian, presumably Picard.

*

Paul Brickhill wrote the first account of the mass breakout from Stalag Luft 3. He was a first-hand witness to the events, but Brickhill may well have embellished his story for dramatic effect. In his book, *The Great Escape*, he wrote about Walenn's moustache … *'a strange face which he recognized after a second or two as Tim Walenn without his great moustache, which he had shaved off for the occasion.'*

It would appear that Walenn without a moustache was something of a novelty or a surprise. And yet Walenn spent many months working on forged documents for himself and many others. Some of these documents had an identity picture which would have been taken using a camera in the camp many months before. Walenn would have been photographed sporting his trademark moustache, and to shave it off for the escape made no sense—it would have immediately aroused the suspicion of anyone looking at his documents.

This moustache is not mentioned in any of the other first-hand accounts. Brickhill is unlikely to have seen Walenn on the night of the escape, so maybe this was something which he added to his book for a little dramatic effect.

Epilogue

This book does not seek to raise a pretentious cenotaph for fifty flying men who, when their own daring clashed with a political decision, became isolated from a hundred thousand other Allied aircrew who died in the Second World War. Rather it lays a lily on their monument dedicated to the patient pursuit of justice which their deaths provoked, and that has no known memorial.

Allen Andrews

*

The team from the RAF relentlessly tracked down, arrested, and interrogated the suspected war criminals responsible for the murders of the fifty RAF officers. The incredible work of the SIB team saw a number of those who were guilty of the murders tried for their crimes.

The small detachment of investigators, numbering five officers and fifteen NCOs, led by Wilfred Bowes and Frank McKenna, was active for three years and identified sixty-nine Germans who had been directly involved in The Great Escape murders.

Of those, twenty-one were eventually executed for the part they played; seventeen were jailed; eleven committed suicide at the end of the war; seven were never traced, presumed dead; six had been killed during the closing stages of the war; six were arrested but not charged, and another three were charged but were either acquitted or the sentence was quashed on review.

The members of the Special Investigation Branch team had conducted over a hundred thousand interrogations and the arrests of those responsible. They established the names of most of the murderers of the fifty Allied officers. The guilt of the German military high command was condemned at Nuremberg by a court which, for the first time in history, was declared competent to try and punish transgressions of international law.

The resounding achievement of the Special Investigation Branch team lay in enforcing international law and ultimately was something of a moral victory. Whether they were able to keep the political promise made by Eden and serve exemplary justice is debatable but not through any fault of the SIB, just the political leadership which lost its will to prosecute the majority of those officials who were responsible for Nazi atrocities.

The Stalag Luft 3 case was the only major war crime ever entrusted to a separate arm of the Service. The Special Investigation Branch men who completed the case were a very small, very independent, and remarkably dedicated team. Their dedication to their duty was exemplary and they deserved all of the honours they received.

Thirty years later Flight Lieutenant Courtney said:

'They left it to us. They picked us, if I may say so humbly, as chaps who would do our best, not out of sinister revenge, but out of a desire to clear it up and with some sense of the absolute in justice. I'm an older man now, and I like to think that that was my ambition.' [62]

*

The story of 'The Great Escape' has taken on a certain timelessness, even after other wars and conflicts have superseded the drama of that bitterly cold night in March 1944. All of the participants who were directly involved have long since passed on, but for their families, these relatives are still connected to the cold sandy soil of Silesia and the fates of those who made a bid for freedom and were so cruelly murdered by the German secret police on Hitler's orders.

Some may argue that the escape made no sense and that it was something of a sporting event—a challenge of daring against their captors—but for some, they had no idea what future awaited them. Should Poles and Czechs have waited for liberation from the Russians? That prospect was probably much more daunting than being captured after escaping, for at least they expected nothing more than to be returned to the camp and spend time in the cooler.

They were both ordinary and yet exceptional men. It was their choice to escape and they deserved to be remembered for their bravery and sacrifice.

---

[i] Archives of the Pilecki Institute. Warsaw. IP/Arch/7/35.8.10.2/756. Access date 23.11.2023. Creator's ref no: B162/27885. Bundesarchiv. Zentrale Stelle der Landesjustizverwaltungen zur Aufklärung nationalsozialistischer Verbrechen.

[ii] Archives of the Pilecki Institute. Warsaw. IP/Arch/7/35.8.10.2/755. Access date 23.11.2023. Creator's ref no: B162/27884. Bundesarchiv. Zentrale Stelle der Landesjustizverwaltungen zur Aufklärung nationalsozialistischer Verbrechen.

[iii] Archives of the Pilecki Institute. Warsaw. IP/Arch/7/35.8.10.2/759. Access date 23.11.2023. Creator's ref no: B162/27884. Bundesarchiv. Zentrale Stelle der Landesjustizverwaltungen zur Aufklärung nationalsozialistischer Verbrechen.

---

[62] Allen Andrews, Exemplary Justice (London: Harrap 1976), p261.

Appendix I

AFFIDAVIT [63]

IN THE MATTER OF GERMAN WAR CRIMES AND IN THE MATTER OF THE KILLING OF FIFTY ROYAL AIR FORCE OFFICERS FROM STALAG LUFT 3 IN 1944

British National Office Charge no: UK-G/E 70

United Nations War Crimes Commission Reference:

I, 5567016 ALBERT ALFRED REGINALD JOHN HICKS, Platoon Serjeant Major of the Wiltshire Regiment, at present attached to the ninth battalion The King's Regiment, with permanent home address at 17 Beaumont Place, Crown Hill, Plymouth, Devon.

MAKE OATH AND SAY AS FOLLOWS;

1.

In March 1944. I was a prisoner of war at Stalag XXB at WILLENBERG, which was about 60 miles from DANZIG. I was then the warrant officer in charge of British Red Cross clothing.

2.

On a Sunday morning which I believe was the morning of the 26th March 1944 a Corporal Becker, who was a fellow prisoner of war, brought me a message that four British officers had arrived in the camp, that they had been apprehended by the Germans and required clothing. I went to the store.

3.

When I entered the store, I found four men in civilian clothes, and their spokesman inquired if we had an escape club in the camp. I refused to make any statement until I had received proof of their identity. After the spokesman had produced his identity disc I was satisfied and told him that we had an escape club and we would do all in our power, to help him and his companions.

---

[63] United Nations War Crimes Commission. British Military Courts (S-1804-0160 -- S-1804-0173). UNWCC10.csv:763 https://www.legal-tools.org/

I issued them with clothing which included battledress and cellular underwear. I did not give them overcoats or blankets in order that I might have an excuse for finding out which cell they were occupying so as to make the work easier for our escape organisation.

4.

The spokesman, whom I took to be the senior officer, gave me to understand that they must re-escape that night, I got into contact with C.S.M. A. Dean of the Field Security Police who did all work in connection with escapes.

5.

Half an hour later I persuaded the Germans to allow me to take the overcoats and Blankets to the officers in their cell. I saw them, and the senior officer asked me for my number, name and unit. Each of the officers was in a separate cell, and after verifying the cell numbers and their positions I took the information again to C.S.M. Dean, who in turn got to work trying to liberate the officers.

6.

It seemed that everything was going well. We had arranged for four substitutes to take the places of the officers, Unfortunately the plan failed in practice owing to the closeness of the guard, which consisted of six unter-offiziers for the four British officers. This guard in the evening of the same day whisked the officers into a car and took them away. I did not see the car leave but I believe that C.S.M. Dean did.

7.

As to the identity of the officers, I do not remember their names and did not obtain their signatures in the Red Cross book. The spokesman had a bushy, black moustache and an English accent. He seemed to be about 30 to 40 years of age although his age was difficult to tell. And I remember that he mentioned that one of the other officers was Belgian whom he introduced to me.

They were all heavily bearded and dirty. They were dressed in rough civilian clothing of the French peasant type. One of them had a French beret on. I think that they told me that they had been caught in the neighbourhood of DIRSCHAU, which is the bridge over the Weichsel on the road connecting MARIENBURG with DANZIG.

8.

Sometime later C.S.M. Fulton told me that the four officers had been shot.

SWORN by the above ALBERT ALFRED REGINALD JOHN HICKS at 6 Spring Gardens in the City of Westminster this thirteenth day of August 1945

(A.A. HICKS)

BEFORE ME

(C. BUCKLEY)

Captain Legal staff, Military Department, Office of the Judge Advocate General, London.

Appendix II

Peter MOHR

As part of another investigation, Peter Mohr gave a further statement regarding his involvement and recollections of the Sagan Case. This new investigation was against the former Kiel Gestapo chief and SS-*Sturmbannführer* Fritz Schmidt for murder.

Mohr had been in the police force since 1926. From October 1, 1938, he had been a member of the Munich Criminal Police and was working there when the war broke out. At the time he was a criminal secretary until 1943 when he transferred to Berlin as a probationary detective inspector at the Reich Criminal Police Office. This is where he worked until the end of the war, and crucially at the time of the Sagan Murders.

He worked for the Reich Criminal Police Office, with his final rank as a Detective Superintendent. After the collapse of the Third Reich, Mohr was placed under automatic arrest because he had been a detective commissioner. He was held until his release in the autumn of 1947. After two more difficult years, he finally managed to be re-employed, initially as a senior detective. At the time of his testimony, he was a Chief Inspector of Criminal Investigations.

Whilst he was held in British custody, Mohr was questioned about the Sagan Case but stated that he'd had nothing to do with the murder of the officers. In the summer of 1947, Mohr also testified as a witness at the military court trial in Hamburg about the events that took place regarding the escape of British prisoners of war.

Transcript of MOHR's testimony [iv]

November 23, 1964

Public Prosecutor's Office Kiel

Present: Public Prosecutor BAUER as interrogator

Employee BENZ as Recorder

Peter MOHR, born on 4 July 1908 in Munich, lives in Munich 9, Kornblumenweg 23.

The Reich Criminal Police Office was Amt V of the RSHA, the head of this office at that time was NEBE. At that time, we always addressed him as 'General'. It may be that he was an SS-*Gruppenführer* or *Obergruppenführer*

*

Amt V was divided into several departments. Group C was concerned with the manhunt. This group, in turn, was divided into departments. I belonged to Unit V C 1. Since the office building of the RHSA was badly damaged at that time, our department was housed in two barracks in Berlin-Zehlendorf. The actual RHSA was based at the Werderscher Markt. The head of our department was the then senior government councillor SCHULZE, whom I can still remember today. I mean, he had the title of Dr so he was our supervisor in Zehlendorf.

I am asked about the further composition of our unit. I remember AMEND, who, as far as I remember, was the director of criminal investigations at the time. AMEND could probably be described as a representative of Dr SCHULTZE. In any case, it was the case that we had to deal with AMEND when Dr SCHULTZE was not there.

On request, I confirm that a certain MERTEN was also part of our department. Today, however, I can no longer say what MERTEN did in detail.

Finally, I can now also remember an employee named BLEYMEHL. As far as I was concerned, however, I would not have thought of this name, the interrogator has just given it to me. BLEYMEHL was a detective inspector at the time. He was probably a little older than me. I never heard from him again after the war.

Mohr was asked about NEBE's adjutant.

I can remember ENGELMANN, although I had practically nothing to do with him. I have already mentioned what our unit had to do with the manhunt. At that time, a distinction was made between the Alpha, Beta and the so-called large-scale search or *Grossfahndung*. As far as I can remember, it was the case that only the forces of the Criminal Investigation Department were involved in the Alpha manhunt, and the uniformed police were also involved in the Beta search. In the so-called large-scale search, every unit that could be used in any way was used, e.g. all police forces, fire brigade, air raid protection, etc. There was a very precise plan for a large-scale manhunt.

Even though all possible agencies and authorities were involved in the course of a large-scale search, this large-scale manhunt was nevertheless controlled by our department. I would probably have to say correctly that a large-scale manhunt was steered by the RHSA, because it was such a large-scale affair that the leadership of our office had to make decisions on an ongoing basis. Basically, a large-scale manhunt was triggered by Amt V.

I am now being asked to give information about the escape of the British prisoners of war officers from the Sagan camp. I would like to say at the outset that a few days ago I watched the two-part television programme 'The Nebe Case'. This show brought back to my memory many things that I hadn't even thought about. Of course, I have also given a lot of thought to this story in the last few days, because I knew that I was to be questioned as a witness to the Sagan case. I will now try to tell everyone what I know about the matter. However, I would ask you to remind me, because I do not think I can say much more about the matter.

*

During the first days after the mass breakout from Stalag Luft 3, Mohr was not involved with the matter. He recollected that one morning, he arrived at work in March, and found hardly anyone in his office. He later learned that a large-scale manhunt had been launched. In general, there were many escapes from prisoner-of-war camps, but a large-scale manhunt was relatively rare. The large-scale manhunt did not always have to be applied to the entire Reich, it could also be more localised.

During those first few days after the mass escape, Mohr had to report to the RHSA at Werderscher Markt, possibly 8 to 10 days after the outbreak. It was during this time that he learned that British officers had been shot in connection with the mass escape. For me, as well as for all the other members of the office, this was such an outrageous thing that I can hardly describe it.

As there were some discrepancies with the names of escaped prisoners, Mohr received an order from NEBE to go to Wrocław to see the head of the local police department. He had been given the task of clarifying numerical discrepancies on the spot at the Wrocław Criminal Investigation Department.

It was the case that at that time the Amt V had figures on captured officers of war, officers shot and urns with the remains of cremated corpses. As far as he could remember, there were also figures on officers who had been recaptured. Some of these figures were unclear and he had the task of checking the correctness of these figures at the Wrocław Criminal Investigation Department. The mass outbreak had taken place in the district of the *Kripoleitstelle* [64] Breslau, Wehrkreis VIII.

I was then in Wrocław and spoke to the head of WIELEN personally. When questioned, I want to explain that at that time I had no insight into the various telex, which had been held by individual police stations in the Reich. I can also state that the individual criminal investigation offices had to send their reports to Amt V as well as to the *Kripoleitstelle* Breslau.

My most shocking impression in Breslau was this: When I was at WIELEN's office, he opened a cupboard and showed me urns containing the remains of shot British officers. WIELEN himself was deeply shaken by the whole affair. He told me that he could not understand why the urns had been sent to his office.

I have just spoken with the interrogator LIBER about the fate of the 80 officers. I know that six of these officers, who were recaptured, were taken to the so-called Camp 'A' for prominent prisoners of war were held in this camp, including members of the General Staff. This camp 'A' was particularly well guarded. The occupants were given preferential treatment. One of these 6 officers, who came to Camp 'A', is working today in Hamburg. I can add his exact address to the file, but unfortunately, I do not have it with me at the moment.

After I had completed my task in Wroclaw, I had nothing more to do with the Sagan affair for weeks. Later, however, I received the order—I can no longer give the exact date—to sort out all the documents connected with the Sagan case that were in the custody of the RHSA. It was on this occasion that I grasped for the first time the entire context of the case. I have seen the telex of the Criminal Investigation Departments; I have seen documents that were originally at the Amt IV.

Before lunch, I said that I knew the name and address of a British officer who was now working in Germany. In the meantime, I have found out that this man is a certain JAMES, who works at the British passport office in Berlin, not in Hamburg.

---

[64] Criminal police station.

When I first got my hands on the Sagan file to sift through and organise it, I found it a desolate mess. In particular, I noticed that there were documents in these files that came from Amt IV (Gestapo). This was extremely unusual. As far as I can remember, it was the only time that documents from Amt IV were collected and stored at Amt V. Among the documents were a lot of telexes that were addressed to Amt V and IV by various Kripo and Gestapo departments. Of course, I can say nothing more today about the exact content of this telex. When I recall all the events, this telex must have referred to arrests and shootings. On this occasion, I am asked about the scope of the Sagan file. These were extensive processes that were summarized in a few volumes. When I am asked from which police or Stapo office these telexes were received, I can only remember Munich with certainty. I don't remember if the events in Kiel were involved. However, I must have had the Kiel events in my hands, because everything that had to do with the SAGAN case had been handed over to me for sorting.

Even then, during my interrogation in the military trial, I was asked particularly insistently about the Sagan order. Without any particular reproach, I can say the following about this today: At some time a telex was sent to the Sagan file, from which it was stated that by order of the Führer more than half of the escaped prisoners of war—or more precisely, the prisoners of war who had been recaptured—were to be shot. Today I can no longer say exactly whether this telex was already with the Sagan file at the time when I first got my hands on this file. Even today, I do not remember who signed this deliberate telex. When I testified as a witness before the military tribunal at the time that this telex bore HIMMLER's signature, then I was firmly convinced that it was indeed so. When I am asked to whom this telex was addressed, I cannot say any more. I am reproached for having named the Chief of the Security Police KALTENBRUNNER as the addressee during my examination of witnesses at the time. That's how I remembered it back then. In any event, it is unequivocally established that that telex referred to the Führer's order.

On request, I confirm that one day I was ordered to the Gestapo chief MÜLLER. To an outsider, the fact of my visit to MÜLLER may seem highly unusual. For an insider, this was the only one who was in possession of the entire Sagan documents and who was not allowed to hand them over. So I personally had to go to MÜLLER with these documents, because MÜLLER wanted to see these documents. The Sagan file was a highly imperial affair. I had very specific instructions on how to behave with *Fliegerarm*[65]. I can no longer say today what MÜLLER had told me in detail when I went to see him with this file on his orders. It may be that MÜLLER had already

---

[65] Allied Air Force.

explained to me on this occasion that in the English parliament, there was a commotion over the shooting of the airmen, and that they demanded an exact account of the case. All I remember is that MÜLLER briefly inspected some of the documents; Then I was released again.

From my memory, I remember that I once went to a conference with the Sagan file, which took place in Prinz-Albrecht-Strasse (headquarters of the Gestapo). I have a memory of this conference because it was interrupted by an air raid. When I am asked about the participants in this conference, I can only remember the head of the Kripo and the Gestapo in Breslau. These two had never experienced a real air raid before and now came into contact with a heavy air raid for the first time in Berlin in the bunker. In any case, I remember that these two were very impressed.

When I mentioned NEBE, SCHULTZE and MÜLLER as other participants in the meeting during my examination of witnesses, that was also my memory at the time. Without hesitation, I can say that at this conference in Prinz-Albrecht-Strasse, there was talk of new telex versions being delivered by Amt IV. While the original telexes were without exception 'Secret Reich Matter', the new messages were to be created openly.

I still have clear memories that this 'theatre' shook me very much. Whereas in the first telexes, it had generally been reported that officers had been 'shot while fleeing' after they had been recaptured, the new telexes were intended to report 'variations', i.e. the individual events were to be described differently.

I could only confirm further details about this conference if the relevant parts of my examination of witnesses at that time were presented to me.

In particular, I know that the Gestapo chief of Breslau made a very embarrassed impression when he was approached by MÜLLER. What I said at the time on page 22 of the translation was also my memory at the time. This whole conference made a very strong impression on me; As a low-ranking detective, I was low down in the Reich Criminal Police Office of the Greater German Reich.

There is no doubt at all that I had a much better memory of the events when I was questioned by the military court because the Sagan Case was only about three years before.

It is quite true that the new telex reports gave various reasons for the shootings.

From my interrogation at that time, I am reproached with the fact that I was later also with the Director of Criminal Investigations AMEND at KALTENBRUNNER's with the Sagan file, i.e., that I only accompanied AMEND on the way to KALTENBRUNNER. I don't know anything about that today. Nor do I remember that correspondence with the British Foreign Office was to be prepared at that time. I have no recollection of what I said about this on pp. 24-26 of the translation. But I may repeat—I do not doubt that the whole thing was remembered in my mind at the time as I have described it.

I am asked what fate the Sagan file ultimately had. I declare that the file has continued to be kept extremely secret. It was quite clear to the UN that this horrible story would be unravelled by the British after the end of the war.

Before the end of the war, we had become aware that investigations had already begun in England. I finally lost track of the Sagan files. I do know, however, that we photographed them again. I believe that photography was taken so that the criminal investigation department could later prove that it was not they, but the Gestapo who had 'got their hands dirty on the matter'.

[iv] United Nations War Crimes Commission. British Military Courts (S-1804-0160--S-1804-0173). UNWCC10.csv:763 https://www.legal-tools.org/

Suggested Reading

The Great Escape from Stalag Luft III, The Memoir of Jens Müller.

Jens Müller's memoir of his escape from Stalag Luft 3 was first published in Norwegian in 1946 with the title *Tre Kom Tilbake*. Müller's story was later released in English and provides a fascinating insight into the events of the escape.

Escape from Stalag Luft III: The True Story of My Successful Great Escape: The Memoir of Bob Vanderstok.

Bram Vanderstok was a Dutch fighter pilot of No. 41 Squadron RAF. His memoir was first published in 1983 in his native Dutch, and later this was translated and published in English in 1987.

The Great Escape. By Paul Brickhill.

Moonless Night: The Second World War Escape Epic. By B A 'Jimmy' James.

James was posted to No. 9 Squadron RAF at RAF Honington. He was the co-pilot of a Wellington bomber which was shot down over the Netherlands and he was taken prisoner. James took part in the Great Escape, and he was one of a group of 12 posing as workers from a local timber mill. Soon recaptured, James was sent to Sachsenhausen.

Lie in the Dark and Listen: The Remarkable Exploits of a WWII Bomber Pilot and Great Escaper. By Ken Rees and Karen Arrandale.

Ken Rees trained to be a pilot officer; flew 56 bomber missions over Germany; was shot down into a remote Norwegian lake; captured, interrogated and then sent to Stalag Luft 3. He took part in and survived the Great Escape. This is a real-life adventure story, written with accuracy, pace and drama.

Written a few years after the escape …

The Great Escape: The Full Dramatic Story with Contributions from Survivors and Their Families. By Anton Gill. First published in 2002.

The Great Escapers: The Full Story of the Second World War's Most Remarkable Mass Escape. By Tim Carroll. First published in Great Britain in 2004.

The True Story of The Great Escape: Stalag Luft 3, March 1944. By Jonathan F. Vance. Published in 2019.

Bibliography

Millar, George (1947). Horned Pigeon. London: Heinemann. Available in a later edition. OCLC 51108963

Brickhill, Paul (1950). The Great Escape. New York: Norton. ISBN 9780393325799.

Brickhill, Paul (2000). The Great Escape. RosettaBooks, LLC. First electronic edition published by RosettaBooks LLC, New York. ISBN 0-7953-0022-0

Younger, Calton (1956). No Flight from the Cage. Frederick Muller. ISBN 0-352-30828-1.

Foot, MRD; Langley, James (1979). MI9: Escape and Evasion 1939–1945. London: The Bodley Head. ISBN 978-0-316-28840-8.

Smith, Sydney (1968). Wings Day. London: Collins.

Andrews, Allen (1976). Exemplary Justice. Lond: Harrap. ISBN 0 245 52775 3.

James, BA 'Jimmy' (1983). Moonless Night. London: William Kimber.

Durand, Arthur A. (1989). Stalag Luft 3. Patrick Stephens Ltd. ISBN 1-85260-248-1.

Burgess, Alan (1990). The Longest Tunnel. New York: Naval Institute Press. ISBN 1591140978.

Franks, Norman (2006). The War Diary of Neville Duke. Grub Street, London. ISBN 1-898697-16-7.

Nichol, John; Rennell, Tony (2002). The Last Escape. London: Penguin. Archived from the original on 20 February 2014.

Carroll, Tim (2004). The Great Escapers. Mainstream Publishers. ISBN 1-84018-904-5.

Rees, Ken; Arrandale, Karen (2004). Lie in the Dark and Listen: The Remarkable Exploits of a WWII Bomber Pilot and Great Escaper. Grub Street. ISBN 978-1-904010-77-7.

Ash, William (2005). Under the Wire. Bantam. ISBN 0-593-05408-3.

Clark, Albert Patton (2005). 33 Months as a POW in Stalag Luft 3: A World War II Airman Tells His Story. Golden, CO: Fulcrum. ISBN 978-1-55591-536-0.

Barris, Ted (2013). The Great Escape: A Canadian Story. Thomas Allen. ISBN 978-1-77102-272-9.

Walters, Guy (2013). The Real Great Escape. London: Bantam Press. ISBN 978-0-593-07190-8.

Dando-Collins, Stephen (2016). The Hero Maker, A Biography of Paul Brickhill. Sydney: Penguin Random House. ISBN 978-0-85798-812-6.

Müller, Jens (2019) Escape from Stalag Luft III: The Memoir of Jens Müller. Greenhill Books, c/o Pen & Sword Books Ltd. ISBN 978-1-78438-430-2

Headland, Ronald (1992). Messages of Murder: A Study of the Reports of the Security Police and the Security Service. Rutherford: Associated University Presses. ISBN 0-8386-3418-4.

Index of locations mentioned in this book

Following the end of the conflict in World War II, political decisions were made which resulted in the repositioning of the borders of both Germany and Poland. Many of those locations referred to in this book went from being German to becoming Polish towns and cities, for example, Sagan became Żagań.

German name and the modern Polish name.

Breslau - Wrocław Bromberg- Bydgoszcz

Danzig - Gdańsk

Danzig Matzkau - Gdańsk Maćkowy

Danzig Langfuhr - Gdańsk Wrzeszcz

Dirschau - Tczew

Elbing - Elbląg

Flatow - Złotów

Graundez - Grudziądz

Groß Trampken - Trabki Wielkie

Konitz - Chojnice

Küstrin - Kostrzyń nad Odrą

Marienburg - Malbork

Neu Bentschen - Zbąszynek

Posen - Poznań

Sagan - Żagań

Schneidemühl - Piła

Schubin - Szubin

Silesia - Śląśk

Sttetin - Szczecin

Swinemünde - Świnoujście

Thorn - Toruń

Willenberg - Wielbark

Woldenberg - Dobiegniew

PICTURE REFERENCES

P30: Gilbert Walenn, courtesy of HSBC History Group Communications and Brand. HSBC Group Management Services Limited, Level 41, 8 Canada Square, Canary Wharf, London E14 5HQ, UK.

P31: Romualdas Marcinkus, courtesy of Nerijus Korbutas, n.korbutas@gmail.com

P34: Gordon Brettell, public domain.

P35: Henri Picard, public domain.

P59: Kurt Achterberg, Landesarchiv Berlin, B Rep. 057-01 Nr. 559.

P73: Peter Clapham Collection. Accession Number: 1994.A.0022 | RG Number: RG-10.232. United States Holocaust Memorial Museum.

Notes